D0481785

CITY ON

ON

Two

TOBYMAC

with TODD HAFER and RICK KILLIAN

worlds collide in a beautiful display

OUR KNEES

BETHANYHOUSE
Minneapolis, Minnesota

Published by Bethany House Publishers
11400 Hampshire Avenue South
Bloomington, Minnesota 55438

Bethany House Publishers is a division of
Baker Publishing Group, Grand Rapids, Michigan.

Printed in the United States of America

Library of Congress Cataloging-in-Publication Data

TobyMac.
    City on our knees / TobyMac with Todd Hafer and Rick Killian.
        p.   cm.
    Includes bibliographical references.
    Summary: "A collection of stories, prayers, profiles, and insights serves as a call to action for God's people to become active citizens making a difference in their communities and their world. Inspired by the TobyMac song 'City on Our Knees' "—Provided by publisher.
    ISBN 978-0-7642-0865-2 (hardcover : alk. paper) 1. Christian life—Anecdotes. 2. Church history—Miscellanea. I. Hafer, Todd. II. Killian, Rick. III. Title.
    BV4517.T63   2010
    248.409—dc22
                                                                                            2010020066

"City is about a MOMENT

A moment that we all
come TOGETHER

And our DIFFERENCES FALL
by the wayside

And LOVE fills in the cracks

And we turn our attention
on what UNITES us.

That's what I envisioned
when I wrote this song.

CITY IS ABOUT
A MOMENT,
AND THAT MOMENT
COULD BE NOW."

—tobymac

CONTENTS

"City on Our Knees": *Divided We Stand* 6

The City of God: *A City on Its Knees* 11

SECTION ONE

IF WE GOTTA START SOMETIME, WHY NOT NOW? *Step Across the Line*

TobyMac Blog: *Does Crossing the Line Mean Crossing the Globe?* 18

The Bittersweet Story of Alexandra 20

Mysterious Ways 26

One Sunday Afternoon in Birmingham, Alabama 28

Keeping a Promise 31

Loose Change That Loosens Chains 37

Love From the Blind Side 40

Allyson Felix: *A Runner Takes a Stand* 45

A Pastor Undone 49

The Way of the Celt 54

Becoming a Living Martyr 60

SECTION TWO

TWO WORLDS COLLIDE: *Out of the Comfort Zone . . . and Into the Light*

TobyMac Blog: *The Beautiful Collide* 72

Of Poverty and Politics 74

What Love Looks Like 80

Through New Eyes 86

Chasing Little Miracles 91

From Comfort to Compassion: *One Teen's Story* 94

Facing the Storms 98

Joined by Prayer 103

Searching for Nadia 106

Awakening 110

"Give Me Souls, O God, or I Die!" 113

SECTION THREE

WE ARE ONE CHOICE
FROM TOGETHER: *We Are Family*

TobyMac Blog: A Family of Humanity 124

The Disarming Power of Peace 126

Charles Spurgeon's Five Hundred Children 130

Prayer and Lightning 133

Prayers That Changed the Fate of Nations 136

A One-Way Ticket 140

From Small Beginnings 145

The Clapham Conspiracy 150

"An Appointment With God" 156

A Miracle on Fulton Street 159

The White Rose 164

SECTION FOUR

THROUGH THE FOG THERE IS HOPE IN
THE DISTANCE: *Hope Is Just a Prayer Away*

TobyMac Blog: *Jaded or Joyful?* 176

Into the Jaws of Hell 179

When the End Is the Beginning 185

New Hope Academy: *A "City on Our Knees" Goes to School* ... 189

Prayer and Faith Alone 194

Jean Driscoll: *The Chairwoman of Defying the Odds* 198

A Word of Hope 203

"If I Can Do Nothing Else, I Will Pray" 205

Hope Rises From the Rubble in Haiti 210

"CITY ON OUR KNEES":
DIVIDED WE STAND

It's all love tonight
When we step across the line
We can sail across the sea
To a city with one King
A city on our knees

WHEN YOU LOOK AROUND THE WORLD TODAY, the division is overwhelming. We are divided along so many lines. Rich/poor, black/white, liberal/conservative, male/female—the list could go on and on. Sadly, within the church you will see the same thing. Baptism, spiritual gifts, and style of worship are just a few of the things we are divided over.

There are elements of society that seek to separate, divide, and demean people, and these forces are at work continually. You can see these forces during a divorce, through cyberbullying, or even in the national health care debate. The bottom line is we are divided. We live in such a self-focused society, continually encouraged to "stand up for ourselves" and "look out for number one," when actually we need to think of others, see their perspective, and look out for those who may not be able to look out for themselves.

Sometimes instead of trying to be understood, we need to try to understand.

That's one reason that, throughout my career, God has continued to put certain songs on my heart. Songs like "One World," "Diverse City," "Colored People," and "Walls" express my hope of seeing humanity putting aside differences and loving well—of seeing people realize that we are better together. We can accomplish so much more in life when we spend our time and energy working with one another, striving for a common good.

One of my secrets to staying sharpened spiritually is walking with inspiring people. People who are in hotter pursuit of holiness than I am. It's built-in accountability or peer pressure turned upside down. They make me want to love God and others more passionately.

I have been very fortunate to see great things happening where I live, in Franklin, Tennessee. God has been doing something very special here. One example is the church I attend, Strong Tower Bible Church (www.strongtowerbiblechurch.com). It is a multiracial church pastored by my close friend Chris Williamson, who has written the book *One But Not the Same*. The congregation is truly a Diverse City, and each week Pastor Chris leads us onward as we learn to walk together in oneness while celebrating our differences.

Then there is New Hope Academy (www.nhafranklin.org), another community in Franklin that you will hear more about later on. It brings together the poor and the affluent, realizing that both will remain impoverished and underprivileged unless they come together and tear down the walls that constrain us.

In Franklin we also have one of the answers to the national health crisis. Dr. Tim Henschel from Vanderbilt Children's Hospital felt called to provide pediatric care to children who could not afford it, so he worked with the community to open Mercy Children's Clinic (www.mercytn .org). Today it is a thriving clinic that has seen over 9,500 children.

Other examples include The Red Road (www.theredroad.org), a much needed ministry to Native Americans, and Hard Bargain Mount Hope Redevelopment (www.hardbargain.org), which builds, repairs, and restores homes for those who otherwise could not afford it.

I could go on, but I think you get the idea. In this day and age when it always seems like somebody is against somebody else, people can lay their differences down, come together, and search for the answers.

The answers don't always come easily, but one thing I do know is this: If we hope to find Truth, we will find it when we come together and fall on our knees.

This brings me to "City on Our Knees." Of the dozens and dozens of songs I've written over the years, this one is uniquely special to me. It says all I have wanted to say in a song in a passionate, artistic way. It sums up what my career, my life, have been about: People rising above their differences and coming together in God's love. People letting down their guard and stepping across the lines that separate us. We become one people, worshiping one God. It's a vision of a dream moment for me. I've been asked "Why should we come together?" In response I always describe a life of diversity in one word—*rich*. Life is fuller when we are together. When I have embraced people who grew up differently than I did, who don't look like me, or who don't have the same financial resources I have, my life has been enriched. You'll see this truth time and time again in the pages of this book.

It's no accident that one of the sections in this book is "We Are Family." One line in "City on Our Knees" says, "We are one choice from together / We're family." I'm a husband and a father, and that word, *family*, means a lot to me. I have my own little "Diverse City." My Jamaican-born wife, Amanda, and I have five Jamerican children running around the house. Members of a family sometimes have their differences, but in a strong family, people are secure in each other's love, even in the middle of conflict. That's what holds everything together. That is the foundation. And that is the image of unity and love I wanted to portray in "City on Our Knees."

Given how personal "City on Our Knees" is to me, you might be surprised that it came to me while I was writing a song for another band. During a writing session in my studio with two friends I write with often, Cary Barlowe and Jamie Moore, I felt something special starting to take shape, but I told myself, "No, this isn't a TobyMac song." I kept fighting what was happening.

But sometimes a song is bigger than you are. So I took a break from writing for the other band, made some coffee, grabbed a pen and paper, and got to work. It usually takes me a long time to write a song. (All together, I spent two and a half years working on the songs for my latest album, *Tonight*.) But this time I literally couldn't stop my pen, and Jamie and Cary were right there with me. I quit wrestling with God and just let Him breathe through me.

And the words started pouring out of me like crazy. It was a fast write. The whole process only took about twenty-five minutes. I was just a vessel, privileged to be a part of it.

This book in your hands reflects the heart of the song. The stories are not mine, but are stories of people who have stepped across their own lines—lines of discrimination, persecution, doubt, prejudice, pride, bitterness, self-isolation, and despair. As you read, I hope you'll be inspired to see how just one person, or one small group, can be a mechanism for change.

This isn't a book of philosophies. It's a collection of powerful stories that show what life can look like when people step out in courage and in love, and strengthen the family of God. I hope these stories will inspire you to create a story of your own.

—tobymac

As we have heard,

so have we seen

in the city of the Lord Almighty,

in the city of our God:

God makes her secure forever.

—PSALM 48:8 NIV

THE CITY OF GOD:
A CITY ON
ITS KNEES

IN THE EARLY FIFTH CENTURY, as the Roman Empire was crumbling and Europe was fading into the shadows of the Dark Ages, Christianity was under attack, much as it is today. Many pointed to Christianity, which had become Rome's official state religion under Constantine the Great roughly a century before, as the cause of Rome's collapse. These critics contended that Christian bigotry undermined people's freedom to practice other religions—or to be subject to the dictates of their consciences. They pointed to the Christian faith as divisive and claimed that its lack of widespread acceptance created the crack that divided the empire and made it vulnerable to barbarian attacks.

In response to this criticism, Christian leader Augustine of Hippo wrote *The City of God*. This book made two major main points:

(1) Immorality and corruption, not Christianity, led to Rome's collapse.

(2) All the world was defined, in essence, by the laws and culture of two metaphorical "cities," the city of man and the city of God. Augustine explained how, from the time of Adam, the city of God had worked to rescue and prosper all humankind. It worked to

transform selfishness, exploitation, and greed—"itself ruled by its lust of rule"—into peace, justice, and joyful communion.

Augustine pointed to the city of God as a place that transcends time and space, culture, ethnicity, and nationality. It is not defined by adherence to a certain set of practices and regulations, a particular way of dressing, or even belonging to the right organization or hanging with the right crowd. Instead, Augustine wrote, the city was defined by an inner pursuit of goodness and outward demonstrations of generosity. The inhabitants of the city of God are those who bow their knees to Jesus and join hands with any others willing to do the same.

Further, Augustine proclaimed that citizens of this city would focus their prayers and actions on dismantling a world of sickness, exploitation, violence, abuse, and poverty—and replacing it with a world of freedom, peace, and dignity. The city of God is marked by pursuit of knowing God and living in His ways.

Augustine wrote, "These two cities were made by two loves: the earthly city by the love of self unto the contempt of God, and the heavenly city by the love of God unto the contempt of self."

The city of God, a city on its knees, is a diverse city, stronger for the differences of its individual inhabitants, but united in its pursuit to establish God's goodness upon the earth for all of humanity. It is a city of prayer, a city of mission and purpose, a city of hope, a city of healing, and a city of transformation. It is as small as two friends meeting together to pray about a private concern and as large as organizations and churches that stand against the ills of our communities and continents.

Augustine had the right idea—it is not about the things that are falling apart, but about our coming together as citizens of this universal city with one King.

I have given them the glory you gave me,

so they may be one as we are one.

I am in them and you are in me.

May they experience such perfect unity

that the world will know that you sent me

and that you love them as much

as you love me.

—JOHN 17:22–23 NLT

When we step across the line

We can sail across the sea

SECTIONONE

To a city with one King

A city on our knees

IF WE GOTTA
START SOMETIME
WHY NOT NOW?

STEP ACROSS THE LINE

Whatever you give is acceptable if you give it eagerly. And give according to what you have, not what you don't have. —2 CORINTHIANS 8:12 NLT

The eyes of the Lord watch over those who do right, and his ears are open to their prayers.
—1 PETER 3:12 NLT

FROM WHAT WE GET, WE CAN MAKE A LIVING; WHAT WE GIVE, HOWEVER, MAKES A LIFE.
—ARTHUR ASHE

*In Christ's family there can be no division
into Jew and non-Jew, slave and free,
male and female. Among us you are all equal.
That is, we are all in a common relationship
with Jesus Christ.*   —GALATIANS 3:28–29 MSG

IT IS IN GIVING ONESELF THAT ONE RECEIVES.
—SAINT FRANCIS OF ASSISI

*He who is kind to the poor lends to the Lord,
and he will reward him for what he has done.*
—PROVERBS 19:17 NIV

I WOULD RATHER WALK WITH GOD IN THE DARK
THAN GO ALONE IN THE LIGHT.
—MARY GARDINER BRAINARD

TOBYMAC

DOES **CROSSING THE LINE** MEAN CROSSING THE GLOBE?

THIS BOOK IS FILLED WITH amazing stories of God using people to change the world. Some stories are more grandiose than others. But stepping across the line doesn't always mean selling all of your possessions and becoming a missionary in a Third World nation. Or spending twelve hours every day in your closet, praying. It's the everyday moments—and how we respond to them—that are just as important.

My tour manager, Ryan Lampa, is a great example. Ryan struck up a friendship with a homeless man named Ron, who had been living on Nashville's streets for almost twenty years. Through that friendship, Ryan became motivated to seek out others among Nashville's homeless community. What he heard was heartbreaking. "We need to be noticed," they told him. "We need to be acknowledged. Most of all, we need to be loved."

Ryan and a group of friends decided to put their love into action by preparing meals for a handful of Nashville's homeless. Soon more people joined the cause, and they added a clothing drive to their efforts. They named their ministry People Loving Nashville (www.peoplelovingnashville.com), and they help feed and clothe about 150 people every Monday in downtown Nashville. And even

BLOG

though they meet vital physical needs for Nashville's homeless, their ultimate focus is more than food and clothing. "Love is our first priority," Ryan will tell you.

Ryan's story inspires me because it shows what can happen when someone steps across the line to share God's love with just one person. Sometimes that one person might not be a stranger you meet on the street. Right now, the person (or people) who needs your love most could be a regular in your everyday life.

For example, when I talk to new artists, I encourage them, "Invade your tour with love." My band, Diverse City, and I have decidedly made this a priority. And that goes far beyond what happens on stage. It might be easy to love an audience who's loving you back. But how will you treat the backstage crew, the roadies, the guy who drives the tour bus, or the other bands on tour in an atmosphere that can feel competitive? If we are loving each other, praying together, and hoping for one another behind the curtain, our performances onstage will simply be the overflow of what's happening backstage.

The stories in this section are all about people stepping out and stepping across the line—in faith, love, hope, and courage. In big ways and smaller ways. I hope you're inspired by both the immediate impact these people made, and by the long-term ripple effects.

IN ALL OF THIS, I SEE GOD'S HAND.
I HOPE YOU WILL TOO.

THE BITTERSWEET
STORY OF
ALEXANDRA

HOW OLD DO YOU HAVE TO BE to make a difference in the world? Wait! Don't answer yet. Not until you've heard Alexandra Scott's story.

Just before her first birthday, Alexandra was diagnosed with neuroblastoma, a disease as devastating as its name suggests. Neuroblastoma, a form of cancer that frequently attacks children, usually starts in the nervous systems or adrenal glands.

The day before she turned one, Alex endured a twelve-hour surgery to remove cancerous tumors. The operation left her paralyzed from the chest down. She spent her first birthday in an intensive care unit.

Doctors told her parents that even if little Alex's cancer went into remission, her quality of life would be crippled. Literally. She wouldn't be able to feel any sensation in her legs or move them voluntarily. Walking, even crawling, was out of the question.

Two weeks after this news was delivered, Alex, after some coaxing and encouragement from Mom and Dad, wiggled her leg. This was a sign of things to come from a little girl with big dreams.

By birthday number two, Alex was alive and active, crawling

about the house. With the help of leg braces, she was able to stand and take a few tentative steps. She appeared to be gaining the upper hand on a deadly disease. Eventually, she was able to ditch the braces and walk on her own.

Within a year, however, the remnants of Alex's tumors began to grow. And the cancer had spread to her bones. Three-year-old Alex faced three surgeries in one three-month period.

At age four, she received intense chemotherapy and a stem cell transplant. While spending a month in the hospital, recovering from the procedures, the preschooler told her mother about an idea she had. An idea that centered on a simple, time-honored rite of passage for kids: a summer lemonade stand.

The proceeds from her stand, Alex told her mother, would go to her doctors, to help them find a cure for childhood cancers like neuroblastoma. As a cancer patient, Alex had learned that every year more than twelve thousand kids under age eighteen are diagnosed with cancer—in the United States alone.

"Alex was smart," her mother, Liz, recalls. "She developed a plan. Keeping the money for herself was not part of the plan. She would give it to 'her hospital' for the cure they would find."

With the help of her big brother, Patrick, four-year-old Alex set up the first Alex's Lemonade Stand for Childhood Cancer in the family's front lawn during the summer of 2000—complete with a big homemade sign. Her parents expected donations in the neighborhood of ten bucks or so.

Alex's efforts raised $2,000.

Alex kept committed to her venture. By 2002 Alex's Lemonade Stand had begun to attract national attention like an electromagnet. Her story was featured on *Oprah, The Today Show, The CBS Evening News*, CNN, Fox News, and dozens of other network and cable TV programs.

Sports Illustrated shared her story, as did *Good Housekeeping, People, USA Today*, and hundreds of other newspapers and magazines worldwide. She made several "People of the Year" top-ten lists. That year the stand raised $12,000. Alex dedicated her 2002 donation in the name of her friend Toireasa, who had died of neuroblastoma earlier in the year.

The next summer brought an Old Testament–style rainstorm to Alex's Pennsylvania hometown on the day of the lemonade stand. Still, people lined up like they were at a rock concert. The president of the NBA's Philadelphia 76ers showed up in person with a large donation. The 2003 results: $18,000.

In 2004, *USA Today* named eight-year-old Alex one of twenty-one people whose lives made a global impact in the worlds of business, entertainment, or sports.

That was the year Liz told her daughter that—given a worsening economy—if the stand raised three or four thousand dollars, "that would be a lot. Even two thousand would be fine too."

Alex disagreed. "She said," Liz recalls, "that she thought she would raise more than that." And this projection was from a girl who had endured six operations and dozens of other treatments over the course of the past three years.

Alex turned out to be right. During the 2004 version of her annual venture, the stand, held at Alex and Patrick's elementary school, amassed $40,000. In just one day. Alex, severely weakened by her disease, witnessed the success from a wheelchair.

But the success wasn't limited to one suburb of Philadelphia. Other people were starting to get into the lemonade groove, mixing up their own concoctions for the sake of charity. The success gave wings to a big hope for Alex: She wanted to raise a million dollars for pediatric cancer research by the year's end.

Alex had proven herself a remarkable kid. But no matter how miraculously things went, a charity based on a few summer lemonade stands wasn't going to earn a million bucks.

Thousands of lemonade stands, though, that was another story. Alex's health was waning, but news of her efforts had spread like seeds in the wind. Responses to a Web site created by Alex and her parents revealed an amazing truth: Alex's Lemonade Stands had gone nationwide and beyond.

As the days rolled by, kids, schools, businesses, and charitable organizations across the country set up lemonade stands—all to benefit the newly created Alex's Lemonade Stand Foundation for Childhood Cancer. Every U.S. state boasted at least one stand. Some had hundreds. Canada and France joined in as well.

Senior citizen centers stirred up gallons and gallons of Country Time. So did inner-city schools and juvenile detention centers. At least one stand was planned and staffed by a band of homeless people.

A month after Alex and her team had poured their last 2004 glass of lemonade, she was almost three-quarters of the way to that miraculous million-dollar goal. Car manufacturer Volvo assured her that it would close the money gap, whether it was tens of thousands, or a couple hundred thousand.

Alex didn't see the end of 2004. On August 1 she passed away, peacefully, with her mother and father each holding her hands. But not before she saw her dream come true: more than a million dollars raised to help find a cure for a disease that took her life. To be exact, $1.4 million.

"What she has done, what she accomplished in her life, still amazes me," her mother says. "She was a girl who wanted all the same things other girls want, but she couldn't have them. So she made the best of what she could have. And then some."

At Alex's funeral, her mom took the pulpit at Church of the Redeemer in Bryn Mawr, Pennsylvania, and delivered the eulogy. "We have heard people say that Alex lost her battle with cancer," she said. "We believe that this could not be farther from the truth. Alex won her battle in so many ways . . . by never giving up hope, by living life to its fullest, and by leaving an incredible legacy of hope and inspiration for all of us."

That remarkable legacy still thrives today. Every summer, more than eight million Alex's Lemonade Stands provide their sour-but-sweet elixir to thirsty people around the world. The result: More than $30 million raised, for more than eighty cancer-related projects. Projects that seek cures and treatment. Projects that make existing treatments available to more kids. Projects that reduce the harmful side effects of today's most aggressive cancer treatments.

And it all started with a little girl, a dream, and the courage to make that dream happen. Oh, and a simple glass of lemonade.

Speak up for the people who have no voice,

for the rights of all the down-and-outers.

—PROVERBS 31:9 MSG

PURPOSE IS WHAT GIVES LIFE A MEANING. . . .
A DRIFTING BOAT ALWAYS DRIFTS DOWNSTREAM.

—CHARLES H. PARKHURST

MYSTERIOUS
WAYS

HIGH-SCHOOL SENIOR KATRINA wasn't sure what hurt more: the smack across her face or the fact that it was completely unprovoked. Completely unexpected. From a troubled girl she had gone out of her way to be kind to.

Katrina thought of retaliating, or reporting her attacker to school authorities. Instead, she committed to keep reaching out to her classmate, just as she had been doing for a long time—even though she knew that her kindness was probably what made her a target in the first place. The girl who smacked her had a reputation for being an emotional volcano; thus, most students kept their distance from her.

But Katrina was serious about living as Jesus lived. So she returned violence with love, harsh words with kind ones, enmity with friendship.

Eventually, the school year ended, and Katrina graduated and headed off for college, wondering if her kindness had left even a faint impression.

Seven years later, Katrina's mother, Vicki, an author and speaker, was ministering at a church retreat three states away from her daughter's high school. Among the women in the audience was Katrina's one-time attacker. The young woman found Vicki after her speech and introduced herself. She confessed that she was an all-around mess as a teen—and that she was flat-out amazed that Katrina hadn't rejected her or retaliated in some way.

Then she told Vicki that because Katrina continued to reach out to her, she eventually reached out to God.

Bestselling author Zig Ziglar asserts, "You never know when one act, or one word of encouragement, can change a life forever." Those aren't just words. They are truth. Just ask Katrina. Or the girl who hit her.

Be kind to one another, tenderhearted,
forgiving one another, as God in Christ forgave you.

—EPHESIANS 4:32 ESV

ONE SUNDAY
AFTERNOON IN
BIRMINGHAM, ALABAMA

IT WAS THE SPRING OF 1963 IN BIRMINGHAM, ALABAMA, and the jails were full. Civil rights protests erupted daily, and every day the protestors were arrested and hauled to jail. Others saved law enforcement the time and trouble by pouring into the jails of their own volition. High-school and college students, the elderly, and even children stood behind bars, in brave solidarity for the cause of equal civil rights for all.

By early May, things turned ugly. Birmingham Sheriff Bull Connor had been content to merely arrest protesters, but as their numbers increased, the kid gloves came off. According to Martin Luther King Jr.'s autobiography:

> The result was an ugliness too well known to Americans and to people all over the world. The newspapers of May 4 carried pictures of prostrate women, and policemen bending over them with raised clubs; of children marching up to the bared fangs of police dogs; of the terrible force of pressure hoses sweeping bodies into the streets.

Yes, standing up for racial freedom and desegregation carried with it a cost, and the cost was escalating. But protesters resolved to stay non-violent as they continued their demand of freedom for all.

One Sunday afternoon, several hundred African Americans

gathered at the New Pilgrim Baptist Church and began an orderly march to a jail where they planned to hold a prayer meeting. Sheriff Connor unleashed the police dogs and attached fire hoses to the hydrants along their route in order to stop them. The two groups soon met. One, a small army of armed officers dressed in riot gear. Some held the leashes of barking dogs. Others wielded clubs—or bulging high-pressure hoses.

The second group comprised men, women, teenagers, and children dressed in their Sunday best, as if out for a Sunday stroll together. Sheriff Connor told them to turn back.

Reverend Charles Billups, who was leading the march, politely refused.

Connor fumed. He whirled around on his heels and shouted to his men, "Turn on the hoses!"

What happened next was a turning point in the Birmingham civil rights story. For tense seconds, the two groups stood looking at each other, neither willing to move. Some of the protesters had fallen to their knees, hands clasped in front of their faces, waiting to be hit with the blasts of water that would send them sprawling for yards. Others stood resolute, unafraid and unmoving, staring back at the officers. Then one protestor stepped forward to continue the journey to the jail. Others followed. Those on their knees rose to join them. And slowly, in various-sized clumps and groups, some holding hands or carrying their children, hundreds of African Americans continued down the street.

Sheriff Connor's men looked on as though hypnotized, stepping out of the way as Billups and his followers advanced toward the jail, their place of prayer.

The jail prayer meeting went as planned. After praying, the protesters returned quietly to their homes. The police offered no interference. No arrests were made.

Those who had been beaten just a few days before were really no different from this group strolling to a prayer meeting on a Sunday afternoon. They all fought for the same cause and employed the same tactics. But for one sunny spring afternoon, something was different. According to eyewitnesses, God stepped in on behalf of a righteous cause and protected His children—touching hearts on both sides of the protest lines.

> Don't worry about your children, they're gonna be all right. Don't hold them back if they want to go to jail. For they are doing a job not only for themselves but for all of America and for all mankind. Somewhere we read, "A little child shall lead them." Remember there was another little child just twelve years old and he got involved in a discussion back in Jerusalem. . . . He said, "I must be about my father's business." These young people are about their fathers' business. And they are carving a tunnel of hope through the great mountain of despair. . . . We are going to see that they are treated right, don't worry about that . . . and go on and not only fill up the jails around here, but just fill up the jails all over the state of Alabama if necessary.

—STATEMENT READ AT A BIRMINGHAM MASS MEETING, MAY 5, 1963

KEEPING
A PROMISE

JIMMY AND CARRIE LAKEY had planned to adopt a child someday, but when they were asked to lead a group of college students on a short-term mission trip to Rwanda, they realized that someday might come sooner than they'd thought. So in the months leading up to the trip, they prayed about it, saying, "We will knock on doors, and as long as the doors keep opening, we will keep going. If not, we will know it is for another time."

Surprisingly, given the complicated world of international adoption, the doors remained open throughout the long process. More surprising still, when Jimmy and Carrie looked separately through the pictures of the children they might adopt, they both chose the same shy young toddler with his finger in his mouth. At every juncture, the Lakeys felt God leading them right to this child. When they were told this boy had been found abandoned in a drainage culvert during an evening rainstorm, their hearts went out to him all the more.

The flight to Kigali with the college students went smoothly, and during a break in the events of the trip, Jimmy and Carrie went to the orphanage where their prospective son was being cared for. When they first saw him, he was playing with about fifty other children on the dusty lot that served as a play area for the orphanage. The Lakeys couldn't reveal their intentions to their prospective son, because the other children would be jealous and it would cause problems for the orphanage, but the minute they saw him, they knew he was the right one.

As they stood with the orphanage director and scanned the playground full of all the other children they would not be taking home with them, Jimmy had a thought. These were their future son's friends, the closest thing he had known to a family. One day the boy would be asking Jimmy and Carrie about what had happened to these children after they had taken him out of Africa. Jimmy realized he didn't want to just tell him that he didn't know. He had to have a good answer for him. He couldn't do something just for this one boy; he had to do more.

So Jimmy asked the director what their greatest need was, expecting him to say food and clothing, something he could address with a simple cash donation. In the heat of the moment, that seemed a reasonable thing to offer.

But the director's answer surprised him. Without dropping a beat to think about it, he said, "School fees."

Jimmy thought about that a moment. "But don't you have public education here?"

"Yes, but there are still school fees we must pay or the children cannot attend."

"Well, okay, how much is a school fee? And is that really more important than food and clothing?"

The director turned and looked Jimmy in the eyes for the first time since the conversation had started. "Look at the children," he said. "They are clothed okay, and we feed them okay. Not great, but it is okay. But we cannot send them to school. Without school, they will have nothing."

Jimmy asked again about the cost of the school fees. The director answered, giving the total in Rwandan francs.

After doing the math in his head, Jimmy was convinced the figure was far too low. Could $1.93 a week really send a child to school?

After conferring with others back at the hotel and in the group they were ministering to, he discovered the answer was yes. School tuition for an entire year was only about a hundred dollars.

That evening, as Jimmy and Carrie talked, Jimmy told her about how he had imagined their son, when he was older, looking at the pictures of his homeland and wondering about what had happened to the rest of the boys and girls he had left behind. He also told her how little it cost to send them to school each year. She acknowledged that without education, there was little hope of these children growing up to break free from the cycle of poverty their nation had endured for centuries.

As the couple talked, they agreed that they wanted to be able to look their son in the eye and say, "We did everything we could for your earliest friends. If nothing else, we sent them all to school."

So they did some quick calculating. They figured out that if they made some sacrifices in their lifestyle, they could cover the cost of educating all of the children at the orphanage themselves. It would be their own personal little "orphan project."

When the couple returned home and talked to family and friends about their orphan project, they learned that others wanted to help as well. The Lakeys' soon-to-be son would grow up in the community they all shared, so they all wanted to be part of taking care of his friends back in Rwanda. And they wanted to do more than just send them to school.

In the months to follow, the Lakeys returned to Rwanda and picked up their son, whom they named River Matison Moise Lakey, and brought him home. The more people got to know River, the more they wanted to be part of helping his former orphanage. Over and over, the Lakeys heard, "You've made a promise to River to help these kids. We want to keep that promise too. What can we do?"

As more and more people asked how they could help, Jimmy and Carrie felt they should formalize the effort. Suddenly, calling it the "orphan project" didn't make sense anymore. So as they put their heads together with others, they decided to call their non-profit venture to help these Rwandan children just what it was: "River's Promise."

Jimmy's business is in concert promoting, so now River's face is often seen alongside that of top artists on concert promotional materials via e-mails, flyers, and concert banners. Several of Jimmy and Carrie's artist friends even banded together to record a CD whose proceeds would go to fulfilling River's Promise.

In a matter of months, the effort raised enough money to send all of the children at the orphanage to school. So the Lakeys inquired about other needs. When they found out that River's old friends were sleeping on cement floors without even a straw mat beneath them, they began a campaign to buy them beds with mosquito netting.

More recently, River's Promise sent money to help orphans in Haiti following the 2010 earthquake.

Jimmy and Carrie are amazed at all that has happened since they made the decision to adopt River. At this writing, River is in the middle of his second year living in the United States and is adapting well to his new culture. It is hard to find him without a smile beaming from his face. He certainly loves having Jimmy and Carrie as his family, but his family also extends to everyone around him, including people who continue to fulfill the promise to educate and care for River's friends back in Rwanda.

Looking back on all that has happened, Jimmy says it was a case of God sneaking up on him and putting something in his heart, something he had never expected to be a part of. But now it is something he wouldn't trade for anything. He says the story of him and his wife shows the power of following God one step at a time, and what can happen when you walk through the doors He opens for you.

He called a little child and had him stand among them.
Then he said to them, "I can guarantee this truth:
Unless you change and become like little children,
you will never enter the kingdom of heaven.
Whoever becomes like this little child is the greatest
in the kingdom of heaven. And whoever welcomes
a child like this in my name welcomes me."

—MATTHEW 18:2–5 GWT

If you spend yourselves in behalf of the hungry
and satisfy the needs of the oppressed, then your light
will rise in the darkness. **—ISAIAH 58:10 NIV**

LOOSE CHANGE
THAT LOOSENS
CHAINS

MAYBE YOU'RE A LOT LIKE ZACH HUNTER. The idea of standing in front of an audience and delivering a speech? You'd rather have a wisdom tooth removed. With a pair of rusty pliers and no pain-killer.

Zach's particular fear of public speaking is spiked by an acute anxiety disorder. The mere thought of talking in front of an audience makes him nauseated.

Funny thing, though. By the time he was sixteen, Zach had spoken to more than a half-million people's worth of live audiences and been featured on national TV. The venue for one of his speeches: the White House.

Zach's journey into the national spotlight began when he was only twelve years old. In school, as he studied the lives of nineteenth-century heroes like Frederick Douglass and Harriet Tubman, Zach noted to his mother, "If I'd been alive back then, I would have done my part to abolish slavery."

One has to be careful about making such proclamations to one's mother. Zach's mom pointed out that slavery is just as much a reality today as it was back in the 1800s.

Zach was shocked to learn this painful truth. "I had all these emotions about it," he recalls, "and I wasn't sure what to think about the idea of modern slavery. I had emotions about it, but I didn't think it was enough just to have emotions."

Zach wanted to take action, but what action? What could a middle-schooler with limited resources really do?

Zach found his answer in the cushions of a couch. And under his bed. And in an old jelly jar. And in a seldom-used dresser drawer. He found an answer that would change everything—emphasis on *change*.

As he poked around his house, he found almost $200 in loose change. Intrigued by his cash-discovery excursion, he urged his school and his church to get involved. He called his mission Loose Change to Loosen Chains. He challenged people to launch their own cash-recon ventures. The funds would go to slavery-fighting organizations like International Justice Mission and Free the Slaves.

The result: more than $8,500, most of it in pennies, nickels, dimes, and quarters.

And that's only the beginning. It has been estimated that almost $10.5 billion lurks in American households. Zach aims to direct as much of that secret fortune as possible to end slavery in his lifetime.

"Anybody can make a difference," he says. "Anybody can be a voice for the voiceless."

And anybody can find the resources to make that difference in the world. Sometimes, you're actually sitting on those resources.

SLAVERY

IT'S NOT HISTORY (YET)

More than twenty-seven million people worldwide are victims of slavery—more than in the days of the trans-Atlantic slave trade.

As many as eight hundred thousand human beings are trafficked as slaves across international borders every year.

Half of all victims of modern slavery are children.

LOVE FROM THE
BLIND SIDE

TRAGIC IS TOO SMALL A WORD to capture the world of sixteen-year-old Michael Oher.

He was one of twelve children born to a crack-addicted mother.

His father, an ex-con, was murdered—shot and thrown off a bridge.

He attended eleven schools in nine years, and for one eighteen-month period, he simply didn't go to school.

He failed both first and second grade; his IQ was measured at 80, which put him in the bottom 10 percent of the U.S. population.

He was in and out of various foster homes, interspersed with periods of homelessness.

When Briarcrest Christian School in Memphis, Tennessee, agreed, reluctantly, to accept Michael as a student, they wondered if they were making a huge mistake. Michael was a towering, troubled African American kid, weighing well over three hundred pounds, in a school of mostly white kids from affluent families.

Briarcrest's motto was "Decidedly Academic, Distinctively Christian." Michael was neither.

Michael's first weeks at Briarcrest were a disaster. To say he failed his tests and assignments doesn't give the full picture. He simply didn't do them. He would stare at tests for the duration of a class period, and then leave them untouched on his desk. Worksheets would end up wadded in a ball and stuffed into the bottom of his backpack. His teachers discovered he didn't know what a noun or a verb was. He didn't know the term *ocean* or even *bird's nest*.

Not surprisingly, Michael would not pass a single class his first year at Briarcrest.

During Thanksgiving break that year, Michael, wearing just a T-shirt and shorts, caught the attention of Sean and Leigh Anne Tuohy, a rich white couple driving to their home. It was 9:30 p.m., about forty degrees, and snowing.

They asked Michael where he was going. He told them he was on his way to the high school gym, in the hopes it might be open. "They got heat there," he explained.

That was all the Tuohys needed to hear. Leigh Anne immediately set about getting winter clothes for Michael. Soon, he was sleeping on their couch. And before long the couple and their two children decided to take the biggest step of all: They adopted Michael into their family.

It was among the unlikeliest of adoptions. The Tuohys' life was crazy. Sean owned more than eighty restaurants and also worked as an announcer for the NBA's Memphis Grizzlies. He lived much of his life on airplanes. The couple had two birth children, including a gymnast daughter who often traveled out of state to compete.

Most significant of all, Leigh Anne had been raised in a racist home. When Memphis schools were integrated in 1973, her father pulled her out of the public school system and enrolled her in a private school.

But more unlikely than the adoption was Michael's slow but steady progress. The Tuohys hired him a tutor, who often worked with him twenty hours a week. "God gives people money to see how you handle it," she explained.

As the semesters passed, Michael's grade point average nudged its way upward, from 0.6 to 2.65. As a junior, he became eligible to join the football team. And there the legend began. Michael, an offensive lineman, possessed freakish speed and agility for his size. He could run the forty-yard dash in just a shade over five seconds, and his vertical leap topped thirty inches.

Soon, college recruiters buzzed around Briarcrest like bees at a hive. Michael had his choice of colleges, but one obstacle still remained. Despite his eye-popping academic progress, he still hadn't passed enough classes to be college-eligible. So after Michael graduated from high school, he was hitting the books again. The Tuohys arranged for summer online courses to bring his grades up to snuff. He finished his remedial course work with almost no time to spare and enrolled at the University of Mississippi, the Tuohys' alma mater, in the fall.

Some accused the Tuohys of ulterior motives. They questioned whether they had adopted Michael with the intentions of grooming him into a football star who would one day bring football glory to their alma mater. (The NCAA launched an investigation but found no wrongdoing.)

Undaunted by the cynical speculation, Michael went to college, hit the books, and played some football.

By his senior year at Mississippi, Michael was an NCAA First-Team All-American. And he graduated with a degree in criminal justice. In the 2009 NFL draft, the Baltimore Ravens picked him in the first round, and he's been a mainstay on their offensive line ever since. Michael's story became the subject of a bestselling book, and later the Academy Award–winning movie *The Blind Side,* starring Sandra Bullock.

The movie celebrates the transformation in Michael's life, but Leigh Anne and her family are quick to point out that when you step across the line in love, transformation works both ways. "We have a different view of life now," Leigh Anne has said. "We view everybody differently. There are needs out there we didn't know about. We were living in a cocoon."

She adds that her family's new perspective encompasses more than race: "We are so much more aware of all people now, and their feelings and their needs. You don't know what the guy next to you has going on. He's got mud on his shoes or a tattoo. We're so quick to judge. We are so, so quick to judge. We tend to put labels on people. You don't know the worth of that person or what they could contribute to society."

Michael Oher would no doubt agree with his mom.

Serve one another in love.

—GALATIANS 5:13 NIV

ALLYSON FELIX:
A RUNNER
TAKES A STAND

THE HIGH SCHOOL TRACK COACH stared at his stopwatch in disbelief. There was no way a skinny ninth grader, wearing big clunky basketball shoes, could run so fast. So the coach asked Allyson Felix to run again.

The watch didn't lie. That's when the coach realized the truth: His new freshman phenom, who'd never even worn a pair of track shoes, was a once-in-a-generation talent.

Young Allyson went on to make it to the California state finals during her first year of competition. The following season, she won the state title in the 100-meter. By the time she was a junior, she was running in large international meets against the world's best sprinters. Despite being several years younger—and much slighter of build—than her elite competition, Allyson left most of the world's fastest women in her wake.

At eighteen she won the 200-meter silver medal at the 2004 Olympics, breaking the world junior record in the process. One year later she captured first place at the World Championships of track and field.

She would dominate the sprints for the next two years, always humble in victory. She shunned the fist pumping, chest thumping, and muscle flexing that often comes with the territory in both men's and women's sprinting.

Allyson entered the 2008 Olympics in Beijing as the clear favorite for the gold medal in the 200. She ran well through the qualifying rounds, but she hit the wall in the finals and finished second again—just as she had four years earlier. She was clearly disappointed but handled the post-race scene with grace.

She credited her family with "putting everything into perspective." She added that high-profile events like the Olympics mean that "everyone is watching you and everything that you do, so I feel like that's your best opportunity to show what you're really about."

But as Allyson evolved from teen sensation to veteran athlete, she decided she needed to do more than demonstrate maturity and grace in the crucible of world-class competition.

For decades, U.S. track and field has dragged behind it the ugly baggage of illegal performance-enhancing drugs. Steroid use (and attempts to cover it up) resulted in multiple disqualifications—and even jail time—for American sprinter Marion Jones, one of the most celebrated track stars of the past generation and someone Allyson idolized as a teenager. Other sprinters have faced suspensions, had national- and world-record times revoked, and been forced to return medals they won.

Tired of the cloud of suspicion hovering above her sport, Allyson realized that sometimes, to step across the line, you have to take a stand for what's right. She declared a low-key but public war on the widespread cheating. She joined an effort called Project Believe, launched by the U.S. Anti-Doping Agency. Her participation has required her to submit to an array of random tests of her blood and urine, which are both inconvenient, invasive, and unpleasant for such a quiet, private person. The tests are risky too. A mix-up or sabotage in the testing lab can derail an innocent athlete's career.

But Allyson determined to restore credibility to her sport and to demonstrate the Christian values her family instilled in her.

"Whatever I can do to prove I'm clean, I'm willing," said the soft-spoken, Bible-verse-Tweeting Allyson. "No matter what time I have to wake up or where I have to drive. I feel responsible to be a role model for younger kids. That's important to me. I hope that people can distinguish my character and the way I present myself."

Allyson continues to present herself well, on and off the track. She won the 200-meter gold medal at the 2009 World Outdoor Championships in Berlin, and in 2010 she anchored the gold medal–winning 4-by-400-meter relay team, which set an American indoor record.

Clearly, Allyson Felix is an excellent ambassador for her sport, but it goes much deeper than public relations for her. "My faith is definitely the most important aspect of my life," she says. "My running is a gift from God, and I want to use it to the best of my ability to glorify Him."

With this perspective firmly in mind and heart, running is the means, not the end. "I'm thankful that I've been given this platform," she says, "so that I can share my faith."

OUT OF DIFFICULTIES GROW MIRACLES.

—JEAN DE LA BRUYERE

You are the light of the world.
A city that is set on a hill cannot be hidden.
Nor do they light a lamp and put it under a basket,
but on a lampstand, and it gives light to all
who are in the house. Let your light so shine
before men, that they may see your good works
and glorify your Father in heaven.

—MATTHEW 5:14-16 NKJV

A PASTOR
UNDONE

IN 2006, PASTOR BRAD RILEY found himself in a strange place—
a red-light district for male prostitution in Bangkok, Thailand. It
wasn't that he was unfamiliar with such places. Over the past several
years he had been actively working with organizations that freed
and ministered to women and children trapped in sex trafficking,
many of whom had been kidnapped into the work and were living
as slaves. It was just that he was only hours off the airplane. He'd
barely slept on the sixteen-hour flight, and now he was suddenly
being greeted by the shocking smells, sounds, and lights of the
borough—taking it all in through the stupor of one adjusting to a
time zone half a world from home.

In recent months, Pastor Riley had partnered with an organization called Love146 to help raise funds for a safe home—a
place where children rescued from prostitution would be cared
for and counseled until they were ready to reintegrate into society
as healthy, independent adults. Rob Morris, one of the co-founders
of Love146, invited Riley and others to see the house and experience firsthand the transformational work it was doing.

Riley had expected to visit this safe house, be touched by the
stories of the children he met there, and collect some great video

footage and photographs to take back to the U.S. to inspire those in his church to do even more. But instead of getting a nice rest and clean-up after his flight, followed by a protected trip to the safe house, Riley and his fellow travelers were taken straight from the plane to the exploited on the streets.

As Riley walked down one street, eyes glazed from the lack of sleep, he felt a touch on his arm. He turned abruptly to face a teenage boy, not much older than his own sons back at home. What he had found so shocking was all that the touch had conveyed—it was coy, tender, and intimate in a way that crushed the pastor's heart. Then, he listened in shock as the teen gently and submissively propositioned him for sex.

To this day, Riley doesn't recall the words he kindly used to send the boy away, but he clearly remembers what happened next. The boy turned, crossed the street, found another Westerner, and propositioned him in the same way. The man looked the boy over for a moment and then apparently agreed. The boy took him by the hand and led him through the crowd.

In his mind's eye, Riley went with the pair into the boy's brothel, into his room, and then through every step of what happened next—images that to this day still choke Riley up to talk about. He found himself trying to get away from the vision, running blindly into an alley and pressing his face against one of the walls, squeezing his eyes shut. "Lord, make it stop. I don't want to see this. I can't look away—let me look away."

With his forehead pressed against the cold stone, he heard God gently answer, *"But I never get to look away."*

In that instant, Pastor Brad Riley's entire world shifted. He had stepped across a line he would never be able to step back over again.

———————— ⏱ ————————

In coming months, Riley would continue to support Love146 and hold benefit concerts and seminars at his church, designed to raise funds and awareness for the cause of human sex trafficking, particularly the trafficking of kidnapped children. Yet no matter what he did, it wasn't enough. It was as if his heart was no longer in his chest—suddenly the things he had done all his life in organizing and running a church were out of context, somehow siphoned of their meaning. For the next two years, every goal or plan concerning his church unraveled. His paradigm for leadership, preaching the Gospel, and even being a Christian shifted to such a degree that he began to wonder if he was losing his faith. He found it increasingly difficult to function in pastoral capacities he had once handled with ease. He felt the only thing he could do was leave the U.S. to work for an organization like Love146 in a foreign country. He brought his frustrations, doubts, and crises of faith continually before God in prayer for more than a year and a half. He felt no sense of relief or peace. Then one day he heard a whisper inside of him, *"Brad, this isn't you running from me. It's me leading you into a greater under-standing of my heart."*

At that moment, the peace that had eluded him came back. His understanding of living the good news of Jesus Christ suddenly exploded beyond the confines of all he had thought was essential before. The gospel was now not just a message of hope; it was the reality of letting justice roll on like a river. He knew he had to now tangibly answer to that calling every day of every week. Otherwise, living as a follower of Jesus was a sham.

Pastor Riley founded the organization iEmpathize, which strives to use the arts to advocate on behalf of trafficked men, women, and children around the world. At the beginning of 2009, he stepped down as pastor to dedicate his full attention to raising awareness of the growing problem of modern slavery—a snare that holds an estimated twenty-seven million people today, a total more than all the slaves that were ever taken out of Africa. Through its presentations, displays, and films, iEmpathize raises money for groups like Love146, which are often so busy in the field that they don't have a regular fund-raising presence in the United States.

Responding to iEmpathize's efforts, a pastor in Denver described the organization's traveling exhibit of artifacts taken from red-light districts and vulnerable neighborhoods and villages:

> It is not more facts or statistics about human trafficking. It is smiling faces of children who are brutalized, the glancing eyes of young men made to perform sex, the names of young women forced into brothels that confronts you, breaks your heart, and disturbs your soul. Yet, through this, and the passionate, broken hearts of the iEmpathize Team the light of hope shines bright . . . for through this experience we learn, not only about the problem, but how we can be a part of ending human trafficking.

Recently, representatives from iEmpathize appeared before the Colorado state legislature, providing testimony in an effort to add human trafficking to the list of organized crimes—so that slavers could be arrested and prosecuted with the same diligence as drug traffickers. Through these efforts, Colorado is now the first state to adopt this statute. Riley and his team hope other states will follow.

The Lord God has told us
what is right and what he demands:
"See that justice is done,
let mercy be your first concern,
and humbly obey your God."

—MICAH 6:8 CEV

THE WAY OF
THE CELT

WHEN ROME BECAME A CHRISTIAN NATION, the "Chi Rho" symbol (✳)—representing the first two letters of the word *Christ*— became the victory symbol of the Roman army and was displayed on their banners and shields.

According to legend, Emperor Constantine was on his way to take power in Rome's western extremities when, in answer to a prayer for God to reveal himself, he and his troops saw a cross in the sky and heard the words *"Conquer by this."* Later, in a dream, Christ appeared to Constantine and gave him the Chi Rho sign, saying, "Make a likeness of this sign, which you also saw in the heavens, and it will be a protection in all of your confrontations with your enemies."

A soldier by upbringing, Constantine advanced his cause with the sword and took these encounters with God as an endorsement of interpreting Christianity through Roman imperial eyes. Christianity was spread with conquest, and the centers of political power would be the seats of bishoprics and church authority as well.

Meanwhile, Patrick, the bishop to Ireland, would take the same symbol to the island at the western extreme of Europe (the Chi Rho would eventually morph into the Celtic cross as we know it today).

Patrick brought Christ to Ireland as a servant, as he had spent his formative years as a slave in Ireland himself. Patrick was the first missionary to leave the Roman Empire since Jesus' first disciples. Because of this, his "way" of Christianity is being reexamined by many for what it has to show us about the true way of Jesus.

When Rome "civilized" a new territory, it marched in with occupying troops, built roads, modernized buildings, set up prefects and governors, and then spread its religion. Patrick, on the other hand, went alone and began by simply praying in a specific location and inviting God to begin working there. As Celts came to Christ, he didn't impose laws and regulations upon them, as Constantine did, but invited them to "put on Christ" and to seek Him above all else. He didn't overpower Ireland with another culture, but instead invited Celtic culture to meet Jesus. What emerged was a totally new type of grassroots Christianity. Patrick pushed the Man more than the system, and Celts were transformed.

The mad, naked warriors of Celtic tradition, who intimidated even the Vikings with their vicious, half-crazed fighting style, became warrior-monks. They were spiritual battlers armed with the sword of the Spirit—instead of one from a blacksmith. They were afraid of nothing. Though they were still rough around the edges, their devotion to scholarship and books eventually made them valuable to whatever society in which they set up shop.

The Celtic monasteries were built at crossroads rather than ancient centers of power. Celtic monks went out into the community to minister rather than separating themselves from the world to seek personal holiness. These monks had as strong a sense of a need for justice as they did for personal transformation through the cross of Christ. They were committed to bringing Christ wherever they went while at the same time seeking the weightier matters Jesus espoused. Specifically, "justice, mercy, and faithfulness" (Matthew 23:23 GWT).

For thirty years Patrick continued his mission to preach Jesus throughout Ireland, despite imprisonments and death sentences, despite seeing his new converts executed, and despite facing constant opposition from druids and kings alike. Yet through his methods, he transformed Ireland in a singular way. Perhaps no other nation has been so affected by one man.

No, Patrick didn't chase the snakes out of Ireland (unless these snakes were symbolic of demon spirits), but he certainly would have sat with you in a pub, sang beside you, and likely changed your life forever.

———————————— Ō ————————————

Perhaps history is always divided into Romans [the Constantines] and the Catholics—or, better, the catholics [the Patricks]. The Romans are the rich and powerful who run things their way and must always accrue more because they instinctively believe that there will never be enough to go around; the catholics, as their name implies, are universalists who instinctively believe that all humanity makes one family, that every human being is an equal child of God, and that God will provide. The twenty-first century, prophesied Malraux, will be spiritual or it will not be. If our civilization is to be saved—forget about our civilization, which, as Patrick would say, may pass "in a moment like a cloud or smoke that is scattered by the wind"—if we are to be saved, it will not be by the Romans but by the saints.

—**THOMAS CAHILL,** *How the Irish Saved Civilization*

The Prayer
of Saint Patrick

I arise today

Through a mighty strength, the invocation
   of the Trinity,
Through the belief in the threeness,
Through the confession of the oneness
Of the Creator of Creation.

I arise today

Through the strength of Christ's birth with
   his baptism,
Through the strength of his crucifixion
   with his burial,
Through the strength of his resurrection
   with his ascension,
Through the strength of his descent for
   the Judgment Day. . . .

Christ to shield me today

Against poison, against burning,
Against drowning, against wounding,
So that there may come to me abundance of
   reward.

CHRIST WITH ME,

CHRIST BEFORE ME,

CHRIST BEHIND ME,

CHRIST IN ME,

CHRIST BENEATH ME,

CHRIST ABOVE ME,

CHRIST ON MY RIGHT,

CHRIST ON MY LEFT,

CHRIST WHEN I LIE DOWN,

CHRIST WHEN I SIT DOWN,

CHRIST WHEN I ARISE,

CHRIST IN THE HEART OF EVERY MAN WHO THINKS
OF ME,

CHRIST IN THE MOUTH OF EVERYONE WHO SPEAKS
OF ME,

CHRIST IN EVERY EYE THAT SEES ME,

CHRIST IN EVERY EAR THAT HEARS ME.

I ARISE TODAY

THROUGH A MIGHTY STRENGTH, THE INVOCATION
OF THE TRINITY,

THROUGH BELIEF IN THE THREENESS,

THROUGH CONFESSION OF THE ONENESS,

OF THE CREATOR OF CREATION.

—FROM "THE BREASTPLATE,"
a prayer of protection that Patrick taught his disciples

BECOMING A
LIVING MARTYR

"**Why don't you give the leadership** of the mission to him?" Rees Howells was dumbfounded by the question. For the past three years he had built this mission in Brynamman, South Wales, up from nothing, working every night, after he finished at the coal mines, to teach God's principles and help the needy in his community. In the wake of the 1904–1905 Welsh Revival, people were hungry for God but had little opportunity to hear teaching about Him because of their long working hours and tough economy. Rees had invested almost all of his free time, extra money, and remaining energy into building up this mission, and it was finally starting to see some positive results.

But now, a good friend who had worked shoulder to shoulder with Rees was beginning to believe that he would never realize his full potential while working alongside Rees. This friend shared that he needed to quit playing second fiddle and start a new work somewhere.

Rees felt his friend was being prideful, but when he prayed about the matter, God confronted him about his own pride.

God's challenge to Rees was clear: *"Why don't you give the leadership of the mission to him? Retire, and be an intercessor for your*

CITY ON OUR KNEES

friend. Pray that the mission will be a greater success in his hands than
it has been in yours."

Rees knew the mission was on the verge of breakthrough success. If he stepped down now, people would believe the breakthrough was sparked by his friend. Everyone would overlook the three long years it took Rees to build the foundation upon which the success was built.

Retirement would be not only a step down from leadership but also a step into the shadows, allowing someone else to receive the accolades Rees believed he deserved.

Accolades? Deserved? Ah yes, there it was, that feeling of pride and self-promotion he'd been struggling against for so long. Rees realized, with a twinge of guilt, that it was his ego holding him back from obedience to God, once again. He knew he had no choice. It took a while to put the ego on the altar, however.

As Rees explained it, "For three days I could not willingly accept it [retiring], but I knew I would be pulled through. It was God's way of working one up to having as much joy in a hidden life as in an open and successful one. If my aim in life was to do God's will, then I could truly say either way would be equal joy."

It was a joy he would very much need to carry him through in the days ahead. Rees turned the mission over to his friend and told him he would pray for success greater than Rees's ever could have been—a decision Rees was certain would be the end of his public ministry.

It was not, however. In the years to come the coal miner with the ever-present grin learned a great deal more about humility and prayerfully serving God than he had in his leadership position. Yet at the same time he saw God move as very few did. It became Rees's habit to return home from his nine-and-a-half-hour shift at the coal mine, clean up, eat, and then retire to his room to spend three hours on his knees, reading his Bible and praying. During this time he developed an ability to discern when God had answered a prayer and when more prayer was needed before that answer would come.

Rees's dedication in prayer was rewarded time and time again. From helping the plight of widows in India to seeing victory in battles in the Saharan deserts during World War II, Rees prayed the prayers God gave him until he received God's assurance that the work of those prayers was accomplished. And whether the answer came into the physical world in a few hours or a few years, Rees celebrated all the same. He had learned that when he got God's word on something in prayer, the matter was settled, though the manifestation of that answer might be for now or some time to come.

In his lifetime Rees traveled as a missionary to various places and saw revival in many of the places he visited. He saw people healed.

In his later years Rees purchased three different estates for Bible colleges in Wales without a penny in his pocket to lend to the efforts. To purchase the estates, just as George Mueller had done, he didn't ask for money except in prayer.

When World War II created orphans and displaced Jews on the mainland, he understood why he'd needed three estates for the Bible colleges instead of just one. He gave two of them over to these war refugees as homes. In the midst of the war, he cancelled classes at the college, and the students and faculty interceded around the clock to end the war and pray for those displaced by it.

Rees taught that there was a difference between ordinary prayer and intercession, a lesson he likely first learned when he turned over the mission to his friend and pledged to pray for him. It would be the secret of his entire ministry and what he meant when he talked about laying down one's life for another. To him, intercession was made up of three things: (1) an intense identification with those you were interceding for, (2) the dedication to stay in prayer until the battle was won and release came into the intercessor's spirit, and (3) the authority that was won when the "intercession was gained."

The highest example of this was when Jesus came to earth as a human being, from the point of being born a fragile infant to paying for humanity's sin with every blow He took, every stripe of the lash, and the suffering on the cross. At any time He could have called more than twelve legions of angels to rescue Him, but He did not. He stayed human, stayed as our replacement and intercession, and suffered every wound until "It is finished."

God is still looking for those willing to stand in the gap for others, to step across the line into intercession for them until the victory is won, and to live a true life of taking up His cross and following Him daily. Just as Rees Howells did.

PRAYER HAS FAILED.
WE ARE ON SLIPPERY GROUND.
ONLY INTERCESSION WILL AVAIL.
GOD IS CALLING FOR INTERCESSORS—
MEN AND WOMEN WHO WILL
LAY DOWN THEIR LIVES ON THE ALTAR
TO FIGHT THE DEVIL,
AS REALLY AS THEY WOULD HAVE TO FIGHT
ON THE WESTERN FRONT.

—**REES HOWELLS,** *in an address to students on March 29, 1936, as Hitler began to flex his military power*

THE
ONE-MINUTE
REMIX

Stepping across the line to make a difference in the world can take many forms: A terminally ill four-year-old girl starts a lemonade stand to fight cancer. A twelve-year-old boy turns loose change into weapons against modern-day slavery.

A well-off family (the Tuohys) adopts a full-grown future football star from within their own community. A young couple (the Lakeys) adopt an orphan toddler from half a world away.

While many of her athletic peers look for newer and more stealthy ways to illegally enhance their abilities, sprinter Allyson Felix runs clean, and runs for God's glory.

A humble and prayerful band of believers embarks on a holy march for racial equality.

What about you? What will your unique story be? You won't have to look very hard for "your line." These things have a way of placing themselves squarely in our paths. The hard part will be taking that first step. May all that you've read here give you the courage and the hope.

A PRAYER
TO START RIGHT HERE,
RIGHT NOW

Dear God,

Like so many people, I love my comfort zone. The well-known routes around my city. My favorite pit stops for a snack. The people who "get me." The situations I can control. The stuff I am comfortable with. I like it when the rewards are certain and the risks are small.

I confess that even when I do make the effort to reach out to others, sometimes I don't reach very far. I donate to familiar churches and charities—in amounts that don't strain my budget.

God, please show me places in my life where I need to step across the line. Where I need to quit making excuses and start making a difference. It might be with a member of my family—someone I need to apologize to or make peace with. Or there could be a need in my city that I can help with. I might even need to jump on a bus or a plane and serve half a world away.

Whatever the case, please give me sharp eyes to see those lines—and the guts to step across them. No matter how uncomfortable it makes me. I know that only you are able to do this. I pray that you will show me, guide me, and lead me by your unrelenting grace and mercy.

Amen.

*Tonight's the night
For the sinner and the saints*

*Two worlds collide
In a beautiful display
It's all love tonight.....*

TWO WORLDS
COLLIDE

OUT OF THE COMFORT ZONE...
AND INTO THE LIGHT

Now we see things imperfectly as in a cloudy mirror, but then we will see everything with perfect clarity. All that I know now is partial and incomplete, but then I will know everything completely, just as God knows me completely. —1 CORINTHIANS 13:12 NLT

DARKNESS CANNOT DRIVE OUT DARKNESS;
ONLY LIGHT CAN DO THAT. HATE CANNOT DRIVE OUT HATE;
ONLY LOVE CAN DO THAT.
—MARTIN LUTHER KING JR.

Love covers over a multitude of sins. —1 PETER 4:8 NIV

EVERY DAY WE ARE CALLED TO DO SMALL THINGS WITH GREAT LOVE.
—MOTHER TERESA

DID YOU KNOW?

The Bible mentions the poor 177 times.
More than one billion people survive on wages
of a dollar a day or less. More than three billion
people—about half the world's population—
do not have ready access to clean drinking water.

MOUNTAINTOPS ARE FOR VIEWS AND INSPIRATION, BUT FRUIT
IS GROWN IN THE VALLEYS. —BILLY GRAHAM

ONE PERSON WITH COURAGE MAKES A MAJORITY. —ANDREW JACKSON

HOW FAR YOU GO IN LIFE DEPENDS ON YOUR BEING TENDER WITH THE YOUNG, COMPASSIONATE WITH THE AGED, SYMPATHETIC WITH THE STRIVING, AND TOLERANT OF THE WEAK—AND THE STRONG. BECAUSE, SOME DAY IN LIFE, YOU WILL HAVE BEEN ALL OF THESE.
—GEORGE WASHINGTON CARVER

Whoever wants to become great among you must be your servant.
—MATTHEW 20:26 NIV

HOPE IS THE POWER OF BEING CHEERFUL IN CIRCUMSTANCES WHICH WE KNOW TO BE DESPERATE. —G. K. CHESTERTON

There were no needy persons among them. For from time to time those who owned land or houses sold them, brought the money from the sales and put it at the apostles' feet, and it was distributed to anyone as he had need. —ACTS 4:34–35 NIV

EVERYTHING STARTS WITH PRAYER. WITHOUT ASKING GOD FOR LOVE, WE CANNOT POSSESS LOVE AND STILL LESS ARE WE ABLE TO GIVE IT TO OTHERS. JUST AS TODAY SO MANY PEOPLE ARE SPEAKING ABOUT THE POOR, BUT THEY DO NOT KNOW THE POOR, WE TOO CANNOT TALK SO MUCH ABOUT PRAYER AND YET NOT KNOW HOW TO PRAY. —MOTHER TERESA

TOBYMAC

THE BEAUTIFUL **COLLIDE**

IN TODAY'S SOCIETY, people often find themselves separated and divided—on the basis of skin color, economic status, religion, age, politics, geographic location, and so on. But God is the Father of us all, and what unites us is more powerful than what divides us. We're all in this together, a diverse community of God's children, and together is the only way we're going to make it.

Amazing things happen when people have the courage to live, work, and pray in the spirit of unity and peace. Often, though, to make these amazing things happen, we have to step out of our comfort zone and into a world we find uncomfortable or intimidating. Sometimes that world is physical; other times it can be emotional, relational, or spiritual.

This section of *City on Our Knees* is about stepping out of a comfort zone and into an adventure. As you read, I hope you'll be encouraged to take big steps in your life. But I'm going to raise the ante. If you're inspired to step out or step up in some way, don't think about doing it someday. Nothing ever happens on Someday.

BLOG

If you've listened to my record *Tonight*, you know that making the most of the moment at hand is a major theme. That's because it's an important theme in my life. I try to write about my life experiences. The changes. The frustrations. The sadness. The great victories. Sometimes a song comes from one of my prayers.

A big prayer for me lately is that we will all seize this moment, right now, and seek God's heart. Let Him change our lives, and the lives of others, for the better. Let's start right here, right now.

Right where you sit at this moment, you can make a choice...

Choose to forgive the person who has hurt you.

Choose to make things right with your family.

Choose to tell the truth that you've been holding back.

Choose to interrupt your life's plans to spend some time serving others.

Choose to pursue a faith in God, maybe for the first time in your life.

WE ARE ALL ONE CHOICE FROM A NEW DAY.

OF POVERTY
AND POLITICS

FOR FRED OUTA, HIS JOURNEY FROM poverty to political power was so unlikely that it can mean only one thing: It was a journey led by God.

Growing up in Kenya in the 1980s, Fred felt God's touch early in life. His mother was a strong Christian who helped found the church that the Outa family attended. Fred was devastated when his mother passed away when he was only three years old, but his father was also stalwart in the faith. "For him," Fred recalls, "the only real passion was for God. He decided to follow Christ with all his ability. For him, Christ was above culture."

Tragically, Fred's father died when the boy was in eighth grade. Once the son of two strong, loving Christian parents, Fred now found himself living on the streets, rummaging through garbage in search of food. "Life was hard," he says. "Food was scarce. I learned the hardship of poverty, the need for education, and the struggle to keep warm and to eat."

While living this bleak existence, Fred made himself a promise: He would rise above his circumstances and, one day, come back and serve Kenyan children, some way, somehow.

At the age of sixteen, Fred was taken in by an American couple who cared for him and eventually sent him to the United States to attend school. In America, he fervently pursued an education. He garnered three degrees, capping off his academic career by earning a Master of Arts degree from Biola University's Cook School of Intercultural Studies.

Fred's next life step was to honor his childhood vow. He returned to Kenya as a missionary, using the fund-raising principles he learned in college to generate enough support to cover his monthly expenses.

Being back in his homeland and ministering there felt like the fulfillment of his life's purpose. "All my life I had prepared to be a missionary," he says, "just a simple missionary reaching out to a community."

It turned out that the community would look to Fred for more than spiritual food. And his efforts to help them would throw him into an unfamiliar world.

In deference to Fred's American education, people in his community of Kisumu asked for his help with their rice production, which they believed was being mismanaged by their government.

Fred knew next to nothing about growing rice, but the university had taught him much about the concept of micro-financing. Using this knowledge, he helped launch a small-scale community rice project. "After just one year," he says, "I saw God's hand on the little money we had earned, and things began to multiply."

The community's hundred acres grew to five hundred, then to two thousand. "As the rice production expanded in the area," he explains, "it was touching individual lives by putting food on the table for families—and also bringing money to families to send their kids to school."

The effort produced something else: a trusted leader for a community who had long suffered under bad leadership. Soon, many in Kisumu were chanting, "Send Outa to parliament!"

Fred was gratified by the outpouring, but he didn't see how the two very different worlds of missions and politics could mix. More important, politics simply wasn't his passion. Thus, his answer to the call to office was a simple no.

"I told the people, 'Let's just do rice production,'" he says. "'We have a church here. I want to do a school here. Let's just do what we have been doing.'"

The people of Kisumu, however, refused to relent. "Every day," Fred remembers, "people were coming to me saying, 'You must run as a member of our parliament.' Not just a few people, but the whole community."

Fred tried to disregard the clamor, but he couldn't disregard a change happening in his heart. As he studied his Bible, he realized that he was being called to "respond to the cry of my people."

So only six years removed from university, the missionary ran for parliament, one of seven candidates in his district. When the votes were counted, the election proved to be a landslide. More than half of all the ballots had been marked for Fred Outa. The other six candidates split the remaining votes.

Fred could only shake his head at the turn of events. "I had no clue at all that I would be in politics," he says. "I never even thought about it."

Soon, Fred had much to think about. He found himself leading in one of his country's most tumultuous times. For many years, Kenya had been known as one of the most progressive and modern African nations. But following the 2007–2008 elections, the country erupted in violence. Opposing tribal groups lashed out at one another, leaving hundreds of people brutally murdered. Thousands more were displaced from their homes. Churches were burned. One of the murder victims was a member of parliament and Fred's close friend. Fearing for his safety, people began to walk him home from work at night.

The violence made Fred wonder why he had ever become involved in politics. Was the decision a big mistake? "When the riots started," he recalls, "I was just crying. It was tough. There was this hope I had of bringing all this change, but when I came to parliament all I got was spontaneous violence across my nation. Why would God allow me to come here and then destroy my vision?"

Amid the questioning, though, Fred got a clear sense that God had blessed his election to parliament. So he focused on using his position to bring peace. He rented buses and drove police to villages that needed protection.

He has also participated in the Hope for Kenya forums, presenting his vision for bringing peace among Kenya's tribal groups, and forming strategies by which parliament could partner with other agencies to bring "reconciliation, peace, hope, justice, and love to the nations of Africa."

One current goal is to bring two other members of parliament on board with Hope for Kenya, then assign each of them to recruit two parliamentarians of their own. "Kenya will be strong," he promises. "We will be a light for the nations to our north, to our west, and to the south."

Today, as he looks back on the post-election tragedies, Fred can see how God has brought something good out of the heartbreak. "There is war in Sudan," he says, "people dying in Darfur. Children kidnapped in Uganda. There was genocide in Rwanda.

"Until this [recent] violence, Kenyans could not relate to the sudden hatred, to killings, to murder. But today, when Kenya sits at the table of the African nations, we now know how people can turn to hatred. We know the pain and death of rioting; we know looting and killing. We hurt with those around us. And we know the path to peace."

Peace is what drives the reluctant parliamentarian. "As a Christian leader," he says, "I want to see Africa at peace. And peace is spreading, but we have to work together—not just Kenyans but the whole world community."

Fred Outa's passion for major political causes, however, will never overshadow the missionary heart that will always define who he is. To complement his work with parliament, he founded the Fred Outa Foundation, which centers its efforts in Kibera, the largest slum in Africa. Kibera's single square mile of land is home to more than one million people. The typical house is nine feet by nine feet. The illiteracy rate is 80 percent.

When he sees Kibera's street kids, Fred can feel what it is like to be one of them. That is why his foundation provides school supplies, food, and medicine to more than 420 orphan students. Additionally, the foundation is building a high school for girls, who are often sold into slavery or used as currency in dealings between families or tribes. Education is key to young women becoming independent, valued members of society.

"My memory of my father reminds me every day to help the poor," Fred says, "to open the doors of my home." This is why his compassion for his country's children can't be contained in a classroom or schoolyard. Indeed, if you visit the Outa home on any given day, in addition to his wife and daughter, you will likely find several orphaned children living there as well.

It's in Christ that we find out who
we are and what we are living for.

—EPHESIANS 1:11 MSG

WHAT LOVE LOOKS LIKE

All journeys that really matter start deep inside of us.
—MICHELE PERRY

MICHELE PERRY WAS BORN WITHOUT a left kidney, hip, or leg. While this is probably one of the most obvious things you would notice about her, it is also one of the least important. By the time Michele was thirteen years old, she'd had twenty-three different operations to keep her alive, got around about as well as anyone else on her one leg and crutches, and was already a type-A personality on her way to being a motivational speaker, a leadership development trainer, a consultant, and a published freelance writer before she entered Baylor University when she was seventeen.

But her quest to know God's heart soon took her on a different path, outside the parameters of conventional "success." From her dorm room at Baylor one Sunday morning, she heard singing and wandered out to see who it was. What she discovered was an open-air meeting under the I-35 bridge between Fourth and Fifth Streets. This "Church Under the Bridge," as it was called, consisted of a crowd of bikers, prostitutes, homeless, and other street people. It was the type of crowd that made the hair on the back of Michele's neck stand up, but she stayed. That first service she sat in a flimsy folding chair between a man who reeked of alcohol and another who simply reeked. As cars whooshed by on the overpass above, she listened to the children laughing in the makeshift Sunday school and the worshipers pouring their hearts out to God. She thought, *I bet Jesus would like it here. I bet He would feel at home.*

Working with this church was the first time Michele sensed that God's love might be best experienced in unconventional places. While she had been an expert at teaching children back home in Florida, here she found the children were teaching her. No formulas or prescribed Bible curriculum was going to reach these kids. It was simply person-to-person *love*—and it was a love she wasn't sure how to express. As a result, her prayers fixated on the request, *Jesus, let me love with your love and see with your eyes. I don't know what love looks like here.*

Chasing God's heart in the years to come, Michele spent a few years in Calcutta, India, and then returned to what looked as if it would be a comfortable life as a graphic designer working with ministries in Colorado Springs. But Michele was anything but comfortable there. Something was missing.

One day in 2005, while flipping through the channels on her television, she came across a program about the children of Darfur. She had stopped at the sight of a Western woman in the midst of a multitude of dark African children red from the dust they were all sitting in. The children were showing the woman crayon pictures of Kalashnikov rifles and their families being torn apart by the war.

One little boy showed a picture of his family running in different directions as birds shot down fire from above them. It was some minutes after the program had ended that Michele sensed the hot tears on her face. She was flooded with compassion for those children. Here was God's heart again.

To make a long story short, thirteen months and a number of small miracles later, Michele was settling into the southern Sudanese village of Yei as the founding field coordinator for Iris Ministries. In this process, Michele had learned a very different definition of home—it was no longer a specific place, but wherever God wanted her to be. God's presence was her home, and her home was in His heart—and God's heart was in the middle of landlocked Africa. All of her theology boiled down to a simple prayer: *Jesus, let me love with your love and see with your eyes. Show me what it means to be an expression of your heart to those around me.*

Michele found Sudan to be a place of unimaginable challenges, overwhelming heartbreaks, and miracles all at the same time. She arrived at the height of the rainy season, when roads often became impassable. On her first trip across the border from Uganda into Sudan, her traveling party—consisting of a rented Land Rover full of five men she did not know—encountered a half-mile lineup of trucks mired in the washed-out roadway. By some miracle they managed to make it across a temporary "bridge," at one point on only two wheels while several men sat on one side for counterbalance and the other wheels hung in midair over the mud. At every settlement along the road children would run alongside the car shouting, *"Kwaja, jibu guruush"* ("White person, give me money").

God was overseeing it all. Within the first hour of crossing into Sudan, Michele had met the man from whom she would rent the first building that would be her mission station and orphanage.

The mission would open with a celebration feast on Christmas Day, 2006. Michele had faith to feed one thousand, for which preparation meant driving back to Uganda—a bone-jarring trip—for most of the supplies and then buying a cow in Yei. The trip to Uganda was always dangerous, as the road was normally patrolled by men carrying an AK-47 in one hand and a bottle of booze in the other. Upon returning she discovered that the contractors she had hired to refurbish the building had left with her money and done none of the work, and the cow she had bought was lost. Determined to go on, however, she searched until the cow was found, and she blanketed the surrounding area with invitations to the celebration. When Christmas Day arrived, the banquet was at first ill-attended, but she sent volunteers out to find anyone they could to come and eat until the food was gone. UN officials and local government elite ate next to peasants in rags. A thousand people were fed, and when they left, Michele had taken in her first twelve orphans.

Anyone familiar with life in the heart of Africa knows that it is a constant test of faith, conviction, and mettle—and that is in the areas that aren't war zones. Though many consider southern Sudan "Christian" in contrast to the Muslim north of the country, Michele found that animism and witch doctors still held a tremendous influence. Most professing Christians still held deep superstitions about the power of spirits and witchcraft. Michele found Ephesians 6:12 to be a daily truth: "For we do not wrestle against flesh and blood, but against the rulers, against the authorities, against the cosmic powers over this present darkness, against the spiritual forces of evil in the heavenly places" (ESV).

Michele quite often finds herself awoken in the middle of the night by gunfire only to find new bullet holes in the side of the buildings of her compound the next morning. New people show up on her doorstep virtually every day—orphaned children begging for money, "workers" trying to swindle her, and sick or maimed who need to be healed. But she is also amazed at how often simple prayers of faith are answered, and how the joy in one child's face can wipe away an entire day of dust, setbacks, and disappointments. Every day brings some new challenge that tests her sanity and ability to face the impossible for just one more day, because she believes in a God who can handle the impossible.

Why does she put up with all of this? Because, for Michele Perry, southern Sudan is the land of God's heart. Her type-A personality had to die a painful death so that she could live as Jesus to a land others have labeled godforsaken. Despite all of this, though, in her first two years in Yei, Iris Ministries took in eighty children, hired a staff of twenty full-time workers, started a school, developed training seminars, held multiple outreaches, and planted a handful of churches. When asked about her "strategic plan" by people wanting to accomplish like wonders, she simply shares the following three steps:

Step One: Every morning wake up.

Step Two: Ask Jesus what He is doing that day—not what He wants you to do, but what He is already doing.

Step Three: Go join Him.

Michele Perry has come to realize that for love to have a face to people who don't know God, someone has to offer theirs. As a result, people in southern Sudan are seeing Jesus in her eyes every day.

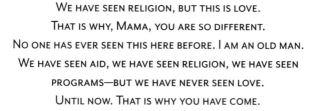

WE HAVE SEEN RELIGION, BUT THIS IS LOVE.
THAT IS WHY, MAMA, YOU ARE SO DIFFERENT.
NO ONE HAS EVER SEEN THIS HERE BEFORE. I AM AN OLD MAN.
WE HAVE SEEN AID, WE HAVE SEEN RELIGION, WE HAVE SEEN
PROGRAMS—BUT WE HAVE NEVER SEEN LOVE.
UNTIL NOW. THAT IS WHY YOU HAVE COME.

—SUDANESE MAN,
to Michele Perry about the work of Iris Ministries

THROUGH
NEW EYES

There are two kinds of means requisite to promote a revival: the one to influence man, the other to influence God. The truth is employed to influence men, and prayer to move God. . . . Some have zealously used truth to convert men, and laid very little stress on prayer. They have preached, and talked, and distributed tracts with great zeal, and then wondered that they had so little success. And the reason was, that they forgot to use the other branch of the means, effectual prayer. They overlooked the fact that truth, by itself, will never produce the effect, without the Spirit of God, and that the Spirit is given in answer to prayer. —**CHARLES FINNEY**

CHARLES FINNEY COULDN'T UNDERSTAND why his words to the congregations of Evans Mill, New York, were having so little effect. He preached every night in the meeting hall there—and did little more than convince a few churchgoers to rededicate their lives to God. On the whole, Evans Mill was a frontier town dominated by its local saloon, just like so many others in 1824 rural New York. Finney was beginning to understand why many referred to the region as the "burnt-over district." Years of self-appointed, illiterate, hypocritical preachers coming through with their "revivals" had hardened the hearts of most to the life-changing power of biblical teaching. Preachers were the closest thing these settlements had to village idiots. They were seen more as fodder for barroom jokes than as community leaders.

Into this scene stepped one Reverend Daniel Nash, who came to check up on the young minister whose ordination he had been a part of. Finney was surprised to see the crusty old minister who had grilled him during the ordination process. In Finney's estimation, Reverend Nash was past his prime, too old-fashioned in his doctrine and thinking, and more ready for retirement than further work in expanding God's kingdom.

Upon meeting Nash again, however, Finney saw something new in the old man. Nash walked and spoke with a new vitality. Still, the younger preacher was suspicious about Nash's presence. Nash explained that he had felt called by God to come and pray for Finney's meetings. He asked bluntly, "What can I pray for?" He went on to explain that he wanted to know who the hardest case in town was.

Still skeptical, Finney mentioned the local barkeeper who had scoffed at the meetings and was known to chase churchgoers down in the street just to mock their faith and shout obscenities at them. Nash took a worn slip of paper from his pocket, unfolded it, and wrote down the man's name. He thanked Finney, shook his hand, and left. He remained in town a day or two longer, but Finney didn't see him again. He heard, though, that Nash was keeping completely to himself, leaving his room only to go on long walks in the woods.

Meanwhile, Finney continued with his meetings, giving little thought to Nash.

What Finney didn't know was that Nash's change in personality had happened from the inside out. Only months earlier, an eye disease had confined Reverend Nash to his room, for even the slightest flicker of light caused him great discomfort. Unable to read, study, or write, the very things he had spent most of his waking life doing, he began to pray. As he did, he began to slowly lose his heart to those who did not know God, so he spent most of his time praying for others. When he finally emerged from his confinement healed, his passion was no longer for the quiet, respected life of a retired minister, but for prayer and for changing lives. So he began the wandering that led him to Evans Mill, looking for "hard cases" to set the sights of prayer upon.

About a week after Nash's departure, the notorious bartender showed up at one of Finney's meetings—in mid-sermon. Muffled whispers drifted through the crowd as the barkeep entered. A few fearful people rose and made their way to the exit.

But the man said nothing. He sat quietly in the back and seemed lost in his own thoughts. Finney later noted that he looked anxious, fidgety. Suddenly the bartender stood and asked if he might say a few words. Startled, but more curious than offended by the interruption, Finney gave him the floor. The barkeeper, with his eyes glistening, began to render the most brokenhearted plea for forgiveness that Finney had ever heard. The man apologized for how he had treated many in the room. He confessed his bitterness and the shortcomings in his life. Then he asked for the congregation's forgiveness.

With that, he turned to Finney and asked how he might give his life to Jesus.

After that, it was like a dam had broken. Numbers swelled in Finney's meetings, and every night many sat at the front of the room, anxiously praying that they might be saved. The barkeeper started a nightly prayer meeting in his tavern. When Finney left Evans Mill six months later, the barroom prayer meeting was still going strong.

After this episode, Charles Finney and Daniel Nash, who became known as "Father Nash" by many, grew to be friends. It became Father Nash's pattern to go into cities ahead of Finney and pray there until Finney came to speak. Nash would stay in town and pray during the initial meetings before moving on to the next town. Everywhere that Father Nash prayed, often with another man named Abel Clary, Finney's meetings bore great results. In fact, in the city of Rochester, a burgeoning young town of only ten thousand residents, more than one hundred thousand gave their lives to Jesus during Finney's nine months of meetings in and around the city. Rochester's streets emptied during Finney's meetings. Shops closed so that employees could attend. Bars went out of business for lack of patrons, and theaters closed or held prayer meetings instead of their usual shows. Crime became virtually unheard of, work by charitable organizations prospered, and it was said you couldn't walk down the street without hearing someone talking about Jesus.

Finney recounted the following story when he was asked about Father Nash:

On one occasion when I got to town to start a revival a lady contacted me who ran a boarding house. She said, "Brother Finney, do you know a Father Nash? He and two other men have been at my boarding house for the last three days, but they haven't eaten a bite of food. I opened the door and peeped in at them because I could hear them groaning, and I saw them down on their faces. They have been this way for three days, lying prostrate on the floor and groaning. I thought something awful must have happened to them. I was afraid to go in and I didn't know what to do. Would you please come see about them?"

"No, it isn't necessary," I replied. "They just have a spirit of travail in prayer."

Bolstered by Nash's prayers, Finney realized incredible numbers of people responding to his messages. And the response to the duo's prayer and unity was long-lasting. Of those converted at his meetings, 80 percent remained strong in their faith and attended church regularly throughout their lives. In modern evangelism, organizers are pleasantly surprised if 20 percent remain true to their conversion commitment.

Father Nash died on December 20, 1831, only a few months after the Rochester meetings drew to a close. Charles Finney, though a successful and highly respected minister for the rest of his life, would never again see meetings like Rochester's. In fact, just a few months after Nash's death, he stopped traveling and became a pastor in New York City. He said it was because of his health, but there may have also been another reason: He no longer had the most important friend of his life and work.

CHASING LITTLE MIRACLES

JOHN CROWLEY'S LIFE WAS WORKING LIKE MAGIC. A lawyer and Harvard Business School graduate, he had a great job with medical giant Bristol-Myers Squibb. He and his wife were also parents to three adorable young children, John Jr., Megan, and Patrick.

Then disaster hit. The kind of disaster that no law school, no business school, can prepare you for. Not even Harvard.

Megan, fifteen months old, and Patrick, just a few days old, were diagnosed with Pompe's disease, a degenerative neuromuscular sickness that attacks the skeletal muscles and also the breathing and cardiac muscles. Pompe's is fatal. The Crowleys were told that neither child would live to see a second birthday.

But the Crowleys refused to accept their children's death sentence. John quit his high-powered job and liquidated his life savings in order to start a biotech company. The start-up's goal was simple: Find a cure, or at least a treatment, for the deadly disease that threatened his children—and many, many others.

The challenges Crowley faced in his quest were many—and mighty. He went from managing businesspeople to managing scientists who are accustomed to having years to conduct and refine their research. But a small start-up doesn't have the time or the money to tread the slow path. It must be nimble and efficient.

Additionally, the side effects that emerged after various high-profile medications hit the market in the 1990s and 2000s had made the government risk-averse when it came to approving new drugs. No one wants the health consequences, product recalls, and lawsuits associated with a medication that is rushed to market. But Crowley and his small team had to balance this reality with the fact that time is the deadly enemy of children like Megan and Patrick.

Worst of all, the passion with which Crowley threw himself into his new world actually took him away from his family. For the first three years after his career change, Crowley's life was a painful irony. To have a chance at saving his children, he had to be away from them about 85 percent of each week.

Eventually, Crowley's company developed therapies that were shown to prolong the lives of children stricken with Pompe's. The start-up was bought by a larger company called Genzyme, which possessed greater resources for acquiring government approval and bringing medicines to market.

Today, Megan and Patrick are thirteen and twelve. (After they survived their first two years, doctors predicted they wouldn't make it to age five. Then, after being proved wrong again, they revised their prediction to age ten.) But the medicine their dad left his career to help develop has reversed the life-threatening enlargement of their hearts. Their mom and dad refer to them as "our little miracles."

Meanwhile, John Crowley keeps working. He wants to find newer, better medicines that will not only extend, but also enhance, the lives of children like Megan and Patrick. He also serves as an advocate for parents of special-needs children, urging their employers to treat them with sympathy and flexibility so that they can manage both their jobs and their extraordinary family responsibilities.

Seek his will in all you do,
and he will direct your paths.

—PROVERBS 3:6 NLT

FROM COMFORT
TO COMPASSION:
ONE TEEN'S STORY

Gretchen W., a high-school student from Minneapolis, chose
to step out of her comfort zone and head to Sierra Leone for
a summer missions trip. Here's her story.

I REMEMBER THE EXACT MOMENT I fell in love with Africa: July 11,
2009, at 10:30 p.m. Eleven days earlier I had arrived in Freetown,
Sierra Leone, with a group of twenty-six high-school and college
students and four leaders. I was sitting alone on the balcony at the
hotel, the street thirty feet below still bustling with activity: car
horns honking, people shouting in Krio, and loud music playing
off in the distance. I was completely exhausted from fourteen-hour
days; sick with a fever of who knows how many degrees; homesick
for my family, friends, running water, and clean clothes; and crying for no particular reason. I was overwhelmed. At that moment,
feeling like I had reached my limit, I thought back on everything I
had seen and all the people I had met. I realized I couldn't imagine
being anywhere else right then. I couldn't imagine spending the rest
of my life anywhere else. The people of Sierra Leone had captured
my heart.

During those first eleven days, and the several weeks that followed, I learned to depend on God for everything—from having the courage to share Christ in a largely Muslim country to our bus not going off the road on the steep mountain roads. In Sierra Leone I found myself praying more than I ever had in my life.

In the short time I spent there, I learned a great deal about the problems facing Sierra Leone, as well as the hope and perseverance of the people. Much of my time in Sierra Leone was spent simply being with the people, playing with children, and listening to their stories. One of these times, when I was in Kroo Bay, one of Freetown's worst slums, I found myself surrounded by a crowd of children, one in my arms and many more pulling at me, wanting to hold my hands. One little boy, who I saw playing among piles of garbage in the dirty water, broke my heart, but at the same time I saw in him the future of Sierra Leone. I thought about all of the children I had talked with and realized that out of the horrors of the civil war a new generation is emerging, one with hopes and dreams for their country. They want to be doctors and lawyers. They want to see their country transformed, not to our Western idea of progress but in a way that maintains their unique culture.

Standing in the middle of Kroo Bay, holding Gibo, I was reminded of all of the children I baby-sat for at home. Gibo would likely grow up not knowing where his next meal would come from, wondering who in his family would get sick from the dirty water and unsanitary conditions, worrying about his home getting swept into the ocean in a rainstorm, and most likely unable to go to school because his family cannot afford the fees. Why should Gibo have to worry about these things? Why can't he have the same opportunities as the children I baby-sat for at home?

As I stood there, holding this precious little boy, I thought of the other children I had met, and about their dreams. Fatsmata, Mary, Aisha, Bao, Rachel, Rosalie, Iwanatu, Memanatu—all of them possess the potential to change their world. I realized that they had entrusted their dreams to me, and that I have the power to make them come true, simply because I happened to be born in the United States. At that moment I felt a huge responsibility to these children. They have everything they need to change their nation and their world, except the opportunity—and that is what I have, what I can give to them. I can be the voice for these children, forgotten by the world.

One of the hardest things I've ever done was leaving Sierra Leone. As I walked across the pavement to the plane, I lingered in the warm, humid night air, taking in my very last moments in Africa. I looked back at the tiny airport with the lighted yellow sign reading "Freetown International Airport" in black block letters, and savored the familiar scent and feeling of the air that I had grown to love. Climbing up the metal stairs to the plane, I felt the weight of my daypack on my back, but I also carried with me the dreams of these children. Sitting on the plane as it took off, struggling to accept that I was leaving the place that had come to feel like home, I knew that I would be back.

SIERRA LEONE
AT A GLANCE

Its capital city, Freetown, was originally established as a British colony for freed and escaped slaves who fought for the British during the American Revolutionary War.

Became an independent nation in 1961.

Was embroiled in a decade-long civil war, fueled by the trade in illicit diamonds—also known as conflict diamonds or blood diamonds.

Since the end of the civil war in 2002, economic recovery is slow, and Sierra Leone remains one of the poorest countries in the world, with 70 percent of the population below the poverty line.

One in four children dies before age five.

The population is 60 percent Muslim and 10 percent Christian. Traditional indigenous beliefs include animism and ancestor worship.

FACING
THE STORMS

"How is it thou hast no faith?"

The thought rolled around in John Wesley's mind again, just as his plate slid back and forth as the sea tossed the *Simmonds*. Headed for the American colony of Savannah as a missionary, so full of faith just a few short days earlier, Wesley now found himself at the mercy of a growing fear that he would drown at sea with the rest of the passengers and crew. The journey had been a succession of fierce storms—and with weeks of travel still remaining, there was no sign of a break in the weather. Though he thought he had been at peace with God, the fear of death now overwhelmed him. He began to question if his faith had ever been genuine.

Wesley contrasted himself with a group of German missionary families also on board the ship. He found himself hungering for what they had. No matter how violent the winds raged or how angrily the waves crashed into the ship, the missionaries' demeanor was the same as when they stepped onto the ship under sunny skies back in England.

Furthermore, he was struck by their humility, quickness to forgive any slight, and eagerness to serve others. As the ocean began to rage, soon after the *Simmonds* had launched, the missionaries didn't become anxious or pester the crew to show them the safest place on the ship. Instead, they gathered on one of the decks and held worship services—singing hymns, praying, praising God, and admonishing one another that they were in His hands and therefore had nothing to fear.

This group of missionaries, who called themselves Moravians, were in the midst of one of their services when a great waved crashed over the vessel, tore the mainsail to shreds, flooded the decks, and began pouring into the lower decks. Passengers and crew alike were sure the sea would swallow the ship. Screams of panic and terror filled the ship. But the Moravians, in mid-song when the storm began, didn't miss a note.

Wesley had never met anyone with such confidence in God, let alone an entire group of men, women, and children who were so unintimidated by death. In their courage he saw the frailty of his own faith. How could he call himself a Christian alongside such unflappable confidence? He wanted what they had; the problem was he didn't know what it was.

John Wesley's mission to Savannah would be a profound failure. Confident in his own knowledge of God and the high marks he had received studying divinity at university, he was baffled by the simplicity of the Moravians' faith. Shortly after arriving in Savannah, he was engaged in conversation with a Moravian pastor named Augustus Gottlieb Spangenberg. Somewhat out of the blue, Spangenberg asked John, "My brother, I must first ask you one or two questions. Have you the witness within yourself? Does the Spirit of God bear witness with your spirit that you are a child of God?" John didn't know how to respond, thinking this an arrogant question for one minister to ask another. When he saw Wesley's confusion, Pastor Spangenberg put it more simply: "Do you know the Christ Jesus?"

Wesley hesitated again, finally managing, "I know He is the Savior of the world."

"True," Spangenberg countered, "but do you know He has saved *you*?"

Wesley responded, "I hope He has died to save me."

Spangenberg persisted, "Do you know yourself?"

John managed a weak, unconvincing "I do."

The Moravian pastor left it at that, but something inside John could not.

Years later, after returning to England a shaken man, Wesley finally found what he was looking for in a service at the Moravian society on Aldersgate Street. As he described it . . .

> In the evening I went very unwillingly to a society in Aldersgate Street, where one was reading Luther's preface to the Epistle to the Romans. About a quarter before nine, while he was describing the change which God works in the heart through faith in Christ, I felt my heart strangely warmed. I felt I did trust in Christ, Christ alone, for salvation; and an assurance was given me that He had taken away my sins, even mine, and saved me from the law of sin and death.

John found what he had been looking for. The seed planted in his heart by a group of families who prayed rather than screamed as storm waters poured into the *Simmonds* had sprouted to full fruit.

It had been a collision with a completely different understanding of who Jesus was, and he read it in their eyes, not their words or preaching. It had shaken his world to the core. But now, through his further searching, Wesley had what he needed to find peace with God—and also to help transform the face of England and the American colonies in the decades to come. A Great Awakening was about to roll forth as the reality of God's grace that Wesley had experienced would be spread to hundreds of thousands.

GOD DOES NOTHING BUT IN ANSWER TO PRAYER:
AND EVEN THEY WHO HAVE BEEN CONVERTED TO GOD,
WITHOUT PRAYING FOR IT THEMSELVES (WHICH IS EXCEEDING
RARE), WERE NOT WITHOUT THE PRAYERS OF OTHERS.
EVERY NEW VICTORY WHICH A SOUL GAINS IS THE EFFECT
OF A NEW PRAYER.

—JOHN WESLEY

A Prayer

May there still be thousands . . . who, in the plan and way

assigned them, and in the orders into which you have called

them, without leaving their way of worship and forming a

new church for themselves, proved their identity as inward

men of God, as members of your invisible and true body

before all people, for your own sake. Amen.

—NIKOLAUS LUDWIG VON ZINZENDORF

JOINED
BY PRAYER

FACING SOUTH DOWN 16TH STREET toward the White House in Washington, D.C., sits an unusual monument to a man who was neither a politician nor a revolutionary. The statue, erected by an act of Congress, portrays Francis Asbury riding horseback, wearing a hat and a cape, and clutching a Bible to his chest. The inscription reads: "If you seek for the results of his labor, you will find them in our Christian civilization" and "His continuous journeying through cities, villages and settlements from 1771 to 1816 greatly promoted patriotism, education, morality and religion in the American Republic." The base also carries the title "The Prophet of the Long Road."

After the War for Independence, the former American colonies were more united in name than in practicality. In fact, the young United States was a hodgepodge of settlements and frontier towns. There were no railways and few roads. The postal service delivered mail only along the most heavily traveled routes. The telegraph was decades from being invented. Thus, communication was mostly word of mouth. And those with the most words were those who traveled most.

Onto this scene came Francis Asbury and the ministers he led as part of the American Methodist Episcopal Church. Rather than being assigned to churches in the frontier areas, preachers were given "circuits" of up to five hundred miles in circumference. Ministers traveled their circuits and were encouraged to spend only a few days at each stop, visiting every settlement or homestead in the circuit at least every four to six weeks. They had no permanent homes and were at the mercy of local homesteaders for lodging and meals. They earned less than forty dollars a year. Most did not live past age thirty-five because of the constant exposure to the elements and the toll that constant horseback travel took on their bodies. But they were faithful in their duties. So faithful, in fact, that it became common in the harshest of weather to say, "There is nothing out today but crows and Methodist preachers."

These wandering preachers—somewhat of a cross between Daniel Boone and Billy Graham—became the news services of the day, carrying stories, letters, and general information from one settlement to the next. They were so dedicated to spreading Jesus' teachings that they often gave up the regular comforts of homestead and family for the sake of preaching and teaching. They prayed as they rode, or read a Bible propped on the saddle horn. (Their horses, having consistently trod the same roads, needed little guidance.)

The preachers became the threads that knit the American frontier together and helped make the United States one nation. They also gave a common Christian language to the American frontier. The Asbury statue was erected as a thank-you to these all but forgotten circuit riders, men not afraid to live lives of constant travel and discomfort for the sake of serving the growing American frontier of the early 1800s.

> On the foundation of a religious civilization which he sought to build, our country has enjoyed greater blessing of liberty and prosperity than was ever before the lot of man. These cannot continue if we neglect the work which he did. We cannot depend on the government to do the work of religion. We cannot escape a personal responsibility for our own conduct. We cannot regard those as wise or safe counselors in public affairs who deny these principles and seek to support the theory that society can succeed when the individual fails.
>
> **—CALVIN COOLIDGE,** *at the unveiling of the Asbury Monument, October 15, 1924*

SEARCHING
FOR NADIA

SOMETIMES FAITH CAN TAKE a person to strange places. In James King's case, his faith led him to ignore police requests and slog through an alligator- and snake-infested swamp, in search of an eleven-year-old girl he barely knew.

On a Friday in early spring 2010, fifth grader Nadia Bloom, who has an autism-related disorder called Asperger's syndrome, ventured into the dense swampland near her central Florida home on a nature walk. She soon became lost, sending her family and friends into a panic. Volunteers and the police mounted a frantic search, but even aided by a helicopter, divers, and trained dogs, the effort was unsuccessful. One day passed, then two, then three. Hope dwindled with the dawn of each new morning. Nadia's parents knew that if she had packed any food and drink at all, they would have been too meager to last. Moreover, any hope was dampened by the fact that the area that had apparently swallowed Nadia was home to thousands of alligators, snakes, and poisonous insects.

Meanwhile, the police scaled back their search and asked civilian searchers to cease their efforts. No one was willing to state the obvious, but the implication was clear: The odds were increasingly mounting against an eighty-five-pound special-needs girl surviving in those conditions for that length of time.

But not everyone heeded the police orders. Not everyone was ready to give up hope. In the pre-dawn hours of day four, James King, a defense contractor and father of five, prepared himself for a compassionate act of civil disobedience. He taped his pant legs to his shoes. He packed trail mix, protein drinks, and an apple—along with two cell phones and his GPS device. And a roll of toilet paper.

Then, as the sun rose, he began sloshing through knee-deep water and muck, determined to find the girl whose family used to attend the same church as the King family. He hadn't been especially close to Nadia or her family, but he felt an unmistakable call from God. *"Find Nadia."*

As he navigated the swamp, King prayed and recited Scriptures. Among those verses was one from Proverbs 3: "Trust in the Lord with all your heart . . . and he will make your paths straight."

As he walked, King felt the Lord urging him to "follow the rising sun." Periodically, King called out Nadia's name, but he received no response.

Until about two hours into the swamp. As he neared a dry patch in the middle of the swamp, he tried again. "Nadia!" he shouted.

"What!" came the reply.

King trudged in the direction of the voice. He found Nadia sitting on a log. She was polka-dotted with insect bites but in remarkably good shape for an eleven-year-old who had just spent four days and four nights in a swamp.

King gave her food and drink, which Nadia inhaled gratefully, although she did express her disappointment that her rescuer had neglected to bring M&Ms.

Then King called 9-1-1 and also Nadia's family. He used the toilet paper to help mark the location. Authorities were able to triangulate King's position by using his cell and GPS signals, and the toilet paper draped about the area helped them target the exact location—which was inaccessible by helicopter. Thus, a team of rescuers had to use machetes to hack their way to King and Nadia, and then carry her out on a stretcher.

"I'm glad you guys found me," Nadia told the team when they arrived, nearly three hours after King's 9-1-1 call. Then began the tedious two-hour slog through thick brush and mud to civilization. Though exhausted, King quickly volunteered to help man the stretcher.

Nadia's stretcher arrived back in civilization, to a waiting ambulance and a cheering crowd.

"Mr. King is a hero," Police Chief Kevin Brunelle told reporters on the scene. "He led us to her."

But King was quick to redirect the credit. "The Lord told me where to find her," he informed the waiting media. "It was strictly the Lord." He went on to reveal that while she was lost, Nadia had recited the same Scripture, Proverbs 3:5–6, that had buoyed him during his search. Some reporters would write this off as coincidence. Not King, or anyone who knows him well.

"He's got great faith," King's wife, Diana, explained to the media. "He's an instrument who was used by God."

And, sometimes, instruments of God can be used in miraculous ways. As a veteran law-enforcement officer, Chief Brunelle has seen missing-child stories come to unexpected endings, both tragic and triumphant. But the saga of Nadia Bloom and James King is one that will forever stand out. "If I never believed in miracles," he said during a post-rescue press conference, "I sure do now."

"Just thank God when you get home," added Jeff Bloom, Nadia's father. "Just give Him the praise for this. This should give everybody encouragement."

The lines of purpose in your lives never grow slack,
tightly tied as they are to your future in heaven,
kept taut by hope. —COLOSSIANS 1:5 MSG

AWAKENING

Morality and religion in Britain have collapsed to a degree that has never been known in any Christian country. Our prospect is very terrible and the symptoms grow worse from day to day. The accumulating torrent of evil threatens a general inundation and destruction of these realms.

—**BISHOP BERKELEY**, *in his Discourse to Magistrates and Men in Authority, 1738*

TO CELEBRATE THE COMING OF 1739, missionaries John and Charles Wesley organized a community dinner at the meetinghouse on Fetter Lane in London. They invited roughly sixty friends, fellow "Holy Clubbers" from Oxford and delegates from the Moravian mission to England. Among the number was George Whitefield, who had recently returned from preaching in America.

It was a joyful evening of fellowship. At midnight the group prayed and sang together, fervently seeking God's will and direction for the new year. As the meeting continued, no one wanted to leave. Then, at roughly three in the morning, people began to fall to the ground, crying and weeping with joy. According to John Wesley's journal entry, without any direction from the leadership, they suddenly "broke out with one voice, 'We praise thee O God, we acknowledge thee to be the Lord.'"

In the days and nights to come, this group continued to meet and pray through the night, calling on God for reform and renewal in England. God answered with His presence time and time again.

Over the next few months, however, things began to change dramatically. The Wesleys and Whitefield had found themselves unwelcome to speak in churches. So one dreary day, in the port town of Bristol, the three of them set up in the town square. Their audience was the yard workers and coal miners on their way home from work. John was hesitant, as open-air preaching was unheard of at the time, but Whitefield had spoken this way in the fields and town squares of the colonies. He found a raised area and began to speak in the dramatic fashion that became his trademark. (David Garrick, a famous stage actor of the time, reportedly said, "I would give a hundred guineas if I could say 'Oh' like Mr. Whitefield.")

When a crowd began to gather, John saw the hunger in the eyes of the men and women. These were people who were worked so hard that they never had time to attend church services, and even if they did, they were generally unwelcome and relegated to the balconies and alcoves, where they would be unseen by the more upscale parishioners. John realized that these were the people to whom Jesus had come, and if Jesus could make a sanctuary out of a mountainside, who was he to scoff at preaching in a public square? It was time to step out of the traditional ways that were keeping God's truth from these who needed it as much as anyone, get over his hesitations, and obey Jesus' commandment to "Go everywhere and announce the Message of God's good news to one and all" (Mark 16:15 MSG).

The following afternoon, the three men found a little knoll outside of town, along the route dockworkers used to walk home. John delivered his own first open-air sermon. About three thousand gathered to hear it.

The trio would go on from Bristol to preach openly all over the British Isles, as well as the American colonies. In fact, the language and fervency of Whitefield would take the American colonies by such storm that four out of every five Americans came out to hear him speak in person. As he preached with style and passion in churches from Georgia to New England, Whitefield helped inform the tone and spirit of America's call for independence from England.

What began with that prayer meeting in 1739 would go on to be known as the Methodist Revival (or, more widely, the Great Awakening), a movement that would change the face of England, as well as that of the land that would become the United States.

"GIVE ME SOULS,
O GOD, OR I DIE!"

WHEN JOHN HYDE'S BROTHER, who had been a missionary candidate, died suddenly, John felt called to cross the line and embark on a mission to India. It was a decision that would have eternal consequences.

So it was that in 1892 John Hyde boarded a steamer from New York bound for India. He was a bit of a misfit as a missionary, somewhat shy and introverted, with a poor ear for picking up foreign languages, especially difficult Indian dialects like Urdu and Punjabi. He was also slow of speech and, to be blunt, a rather poor preacher.

But he had a pair of piercing blue eyes that seemed to penetrate almost instantly to the innermost parts of one's soul. He offered unique perspectives, and he would prove to be anything but a conventional missionary in his nearly two decades in India.

Upon arriving, he was assigned to a language class—which he chose not to attend after only a few lessons. He decided to spend that time in Bible study instead. When he was reprimanded by the committee in charge of his mission, he replied, "First things first." He felt he needed to be better acquainted with the language of God before the language of the locals. The studying soon gave him a quiet, confident teaching style that people found captivating.

Hyde had his first taste of success as a missionary three years into his venture. As he ministered with another missionary, named Martin, a small revival broke out. However, these newly saved people were quickly disowned by their families. Some were threatened, and one person was severely beaten. Thus, the meetings stopped for fear of further reprisals. Hyde and Martin were unsure how to work in such a hostile environment. So Hyde did the only thing that made sense to him: He fell to his knees and began to pray.

As he continued to serve in India, Hyde became a man of intense prayer, and the more he prayed, the more he saw that prayer was the only way to truly reach the Indian people. So convinced of prayer's importance, Hyde organized an annual prayer meeting in the village of Sialkot. It was designed to rejuvenate the Christian workers—both native and foreign—throughout India. At the first gathering, held in 1904, attendees were asked to answer a series of five questions in order to be part of the Punjab Prayer Union—a group committed to intercessory prayer for all of India. The questions:

(1) Are you praying for quickening in your own life, in the life of your fellow workers, and in the church?

(2) Are you longing for greater power of the Holy Spirit in your own life and work, and are you convinced that you cannot go on without this power?

(3) Will you pray that you may not be ashamed of Jesus?

(4) Do you believe that prayer is the great means for securing this spiritual awakening?

(5) Will you set apart one half hour each day as soon after noon

as possible to pray for this awakening, and are you willing to pray till the awakening comes?

By the prayer convention of 1908, John's prayers took on a remarkably bolder and more specific slant: John asked God for one soul a day to be saved—an unprecedented number in such a hostile country, especially for a man who typically evangelized one person at a time. Every night, Hyde prayed until he had the assurance that someone would be saved. The next day he would find that person and lead him or her to Jesus. Every night he cried out, "Father, give me these souls, or I die!" A fellow worker described his method:

> He would engage a man in a talk about his salvation. By and by he would have his hands on the man's shoulders, looking him very earnestly in the eye. Soon he would get the man on his knees confessing his sins and seeking salvation. Such a one he would baptize in the village, by the roadside, or anywhere.
>
> I once attended one of his conventions for Christians. He would meet his converts as they came in, and embrace them in the Oriental style, laying his hand first on one shoulder and then the other. Indeed, his embraces were so loving that he got nearly all to give like embraces to Christians, and those, too, of the lowest caste.

By the end of 1908, more than four hundred had been saved through Hyde's personal ministry.

At the convention in 1909, he began praying for two a day to be saved. By the convention of 1910, more than eight hundred came to Jesus that year, as part of Hyde's personal ministry. As his covenant of prayer with God for 1910, he asked for four a day to be brought to a saving knowledge of Jesus Christ, to confess Christ in public, and to be baptized in His name.

Any day that Hyde did not bring four souls into the kingdom, he felt a weight on his heart, a weight so heavy that he couldn't eat or sleep. When he prayed and asked God to reveal what was blocking his prayers, the answer would invariably come to him. Often, Hyde would realize the lack of praise in his own life. Then he would confess his sins, accept God's forgiveness, and ask for the spirit of praise—in the same way he might ask for the fruit of the Spirit to grow in his life. He would lose himself—and his aches and mourning—in God's joy as he sang. He praised God for His power to bring souls to him, and the number he was missing for that day would be made up the next.

Just after the 1910 Sialkot convention, Hyde came down with a fever while visiting friends in Calcutta. When a doctor called on him, he found Hyde in serious condition. He was recalled from the mission field, and a tumor was discovered in his brain. When doctors operated on him, they found the tumor to be a malignant sarcoma—an untreatable cancer at the time.

Thus, John "Praying" Hyde, as those who knew him in India had come to call him, died on February 17, 1912, at age forty-seven. His last words were, *"Bol, Yisu' Masih, Ki Jai,"* which, translated from Punjabi means, "Shout, the victory of Jesus Christ!"

> The renewal of the Church will depend on the renewal of our prayer life. The powers of the world to come are at our disposal if we will make time for quiet hours for fellowship and communion [with Jesus in prayer], which is our Lord's supreme yearning desire.
>
> **—FRANCIS A. MCGAW,** *personal friend and biographer of John Hyde*

THE ONE-MINUTE REMIX

God can do amazing things through us when we're willing to step beyond our comfort zone and venture into new worlds. True, it can be hard for us to adjust to these new worlds, and it can be a challenge for those in these worlds to adjust to us—whether it's the different worlds of culture and race or the kingdom of God colliding with the kingdom of this world, when love collides with hatred, materialism, and selfishness.

But the results can be beautiful. John Crowley left his comfortable career but discovered treatments for a disease that threatens the lives of thousands of children.

For Fred Outa, missions, not politics, was his passion, but he found a way to bring his missionary heart into the often-corrupt and inefficient political arena. As a result, he is transforming a community, a country, and an entire continent.

James King trudged his way through a gator-infested swamp, searching for a girl he barely knew. Guided by prayer, he found her, long after the professional rescue teams had all but given up hope.

Faith is at its best when it's on the move, leading people to places they never thought they'd go, and changing lives for the better. The next time you're given a chance to follow your faith, wherever it may take you, will you choose to move?

A PRAYER
FOR COURAGE

This section's closing prayer comes courtesy of Saint Ignatius of Loyola, a sixteenth-century Spanish knight who dedicated his life to Jesus after being seriously wounded in battle at age thirty. Saint Ignatius was a fierce man of prayer, often spending seven hours a day communing with his Lord.

> LORD JESUS, TEACH ME TO BE GENEROUS;
> TEACH ME TO SERVE YOU AS YOU DESERVE,
> TO GIVE AND NOT TO COUNT THE COST,
> TO FIGHT AND NOT TO HEED THE WOUNDS,
> TO TOIL AND NOT TO SEEK FOR REST,
> TO LABOR AND NOT TO SEEK REWARD,
> EXCEPT THAT OF KNOWING THAT I DO YOUR WILL.
> AMEN.

From cathedrals to Third World missions

Love will fall to the earth

Like a crashing wave.

WE ARE ONE
CHOICE FROM
TOGETHER

WE ARE FAMILY

In Christ's family there can be no division into Jew and non-Jew, slave and free, male and female. Among us you are all equal. That is, we are all in a common relationship with Jesus Christ.

—GALATIANS 3:28–29 MSG

Never walk away from someone who deserves help; your hand is God's hand for that person. **—PROVERBS 3:27 MSG**

FOR A COMMUNITY TO BE WHOLE AND HEALTHY, IT MUST BE BASED ON PEOPLE'S LOVE AND CONCERN FOR EACH OTHER.

—MILLARD FULLER, *founder of Habitat for Humanity*

Dear friends, let us love one another, for love comes from God.

—1 JOHN 4:7 NIV

Speak up for the people who have no voice, for the rights of all the down-and-outers. **—PROVERBS 31:9 MSG**

*How great is the love the Father has lavished on us, that we
should be called children of God! And that is what we are!*
—1 JOHN 3:1 NIV

*Remember those who are mistreated as if you were being
mistreated.* —HEBREWS 13:3 GWT

*Love each other as brothers and sisters and honor others
more than you do yourself.* —ROMANS 12:10 CEV

TOBYMAC

A FAMILY **OF HUMANITY**

I RECENTLY RECEIVED a letter from a woman on the brink of divorce. Or, more accurately, over the brink of divorce. She had just walked out of a marriage-counseling session with her husband, completely resolved to end her marriage. She got in her car and sped away.

On the car radio, a song was playing. One of my songs, "City on Our Knees."

Now, anyone who has heard this song knows it's not about marriage reconciliation, but when this woman heard the lyrics "If you gotta start somewhere, why not here / If you gotta start sometime, why not now," something happened. God used those words and the spirit of the music, somehow, to change her heart.

She started crying and committed to trying again to heal her marriage. When I received the letter from this woman, it touched me. When I read letters like this, when I see God move on people's hearts when tragedies happen or just when people reach out to people in need, I am more hopeful than ever about people coming together. About humanity loving well.

I am fortunate to be able to see God moving in some of the people right around me—people who are making choices daily to bring people together.

One of those people is Susannah Parrish, a graphic designer who has done a lot of artwork and design for us over the years. During the Nashville floods in May 2010, Susannah was inspired to design a T-shirt that she could sell to raise money for the relief efforts. She thought she might sell

a few shirts to friends and friends of friends. But the design caught on—in fact, within days it caught the attention of more than twenty-five thousand people on Facebook. Susannah never dreamed her small effort would make such a difference, but her Nashville Flood Tees (www.nashvillefloodtees .com) went on to sell more than eighteen thousand shirts, enabling her to donate over two hundred thousand dollars to various relief organizations in the Nashville area.

One key to humanity's loving well, as Susannah has shown, is realizing that we are family; we are parts of a body, and each part is needed. Sometimes, when one part of the body is weak, fatigued, or injured, the other parts have to kick in and help out. Susannah saw herself as one small, humble part of the body, but her unique artistic skill led to a much greater result than she could have imagined.

Once Susannah's design hit Facebook, thousands of people—of differing ages, races, and religious backgrounds—acted like the body's nerve endings, passing on the message from one cell to another.

It's our differences that make us effective, our differences that make us rich. All we have to do is work together toward a common good. The stories in this section demonstrate just that.

I am encouraged when I see humanity move further away from our historical mistakes. I am encouraged when I see parts of the body that are injured, weak, or neglected receiving care instead of ridicule. I am encouraged when I see communities and families moving further away from the old patterns and honestly asking themselves, "What does real love look like?"

THE DISARMING POWER OF PEACE

TERRY DOBSON FLEW TO JAPAN with a singular purpose: to be one of the first Americans to study the martial art of aikido, in the land where it was invented. In Japan, Dobson trained eight hours a day, honing his skills and building his muscles. Soon, he was in the best shape of his life, the proverbial "man you wouldn't want to mess with."

After training one afternoon, Dobson took the train home. At a stop, a large and obviously drunk laborer boarded the train. This man was an angry drunk. He began screaming at random passengers. He even took a swing at a woman holding a baby. She fell back into the laps of an elderly couple as she dodged the blow, and chaos erupted as passengers scrambled to the back of the train. As people dodged past him, the drunk swung again and again. Fortunately, he was so drunk that none of his punches found a target. Frustrated, the man grabbed a metal pole in the middle of the car and focused all of his rage on trying to rip it from its moorings.

At this point, Dobson decided to put his martial arts training into practice and confront the man before he hurt someone. He remembered the words of his teacher: *"Aikido is the art of reconciliation. . . . If you try to dominate people, you are already defeated. We study how to resolve conflict, not how to start it."*

In this spirit, Dobson was committed to use his skills only in defense, and here was an opportunity to defend a whole train full of people. He wasn't itching for a fight, but it would be negligent, he reasoned, to continue to be a spectator. So, while everyone else was either fleeing or cowering, Dobson rose slowly from his seat and moved toward the belligerent man.

Seeing him, the drunk roared, "Aha! A foreigner! You need a lesson in Japanese manners!" A titanic clash seemed inevitable.

Suddenly, though, Dobson was stopped cold by a loud, "Hey!"

The call wasn't hostile; it was offered as a boisterous greeting to an old friend. Shocked, Dobson saw the drunken man whirl to face the source of the greeting—an elderly man, probably in his seventies, dressed in a traditional kimono and sitting not far from where the workman had boarded the train. The old man grinned as he waved at the drunk and offered a joyful, "C'mere."

Puzzled, the drunk took a tentative step toward the old man. "Why should I talk to you?" he asked suspiciously.

Meanwhile, Dobson closed in on the drunk, ready to drop him if he attacked.

"What'cha been drinking?" the old man inquired, still beaming.

"I've been drinking sake, and it's none of your business," came the snarling reply.

"Oh, that's wonderful, absolutely wonderful," the old man

observed warmly. "You see, I love sake too. Every night, me and my wife—she's sixty-seven, you know—we warm up a little bottle of sake and take it out into the garden, and we sit on a wooden bench. . . ."

The man in the kimono went on to describe the peaceful beauty of their garden, including a cherished persimmon tree and the enjoyment he and his wife got from sitting there, drinking sake together.

As he listened, the workman's fists unclenched. His shoulders relaxed. "Yeah . . . I love persimmons too," he said slowly.

"Yes," said the old man, "and I am sure you have a wonderful wife."

The workman looked wounded. "No," he answered, "my wife died." Tears welled in his eyes. Sobs convulsed his body. He began to explain how his wife had died. Then, he revealed, he had lost his home, his job, and, finally, his self-esteem.

After watching the encounter for some time, Dobson looked up to see that the train was arriving at his stop. The drunk was now sprawled across a seat, his head in the man's lap, weeping. Tenderly, the older man comforted him, not as a dangerous drunk but as a troubled son. Dobson heard the old man invite the laborer to come home with him and tell him more of his story.

Then Dobson stepped off the train and headed to his apartment. He had spent hundreds of hours learning a martial art, but he had just witnessed a much more powerful discipline: the art of using fatherly patience, grace, and love to calm the raging storm inside a troubled man. A man who, at first glance, appeared to be looking for a fight. But what he was really looking for was family.

You have heard that it was said, "An eye for an eye
and a tooth for a tooth." But I say to you,
Do not resist the one who is evil.
But if anyone slaps you on the right cheek,
turn to him the other also.
And if anyone would sue you and take your tunic,
let him have your cloak as well.
And if anyone forces you to go one mile,
go with him two miles.
Give to the one who begs from you, and do not refuse
the one who would borrow from you.

—MATTHEW 5:38–42 ESV

CHARLES SPURGEON'S
FIVE HUNDRED
CHILDREN

THE FAMED NINETEENTH-CENTURY ENGLISH PREACHER Charles Spurgeon was a rock star before the term was invented. He started preaching at age sixteen and headed his first church at nineteen. By age twenty-two he was regularly drawing more than ten thousand people to hear him speak. Circus pioneer P. T. Barnum even tried to hire Spurgeon to tour with him. (The preacher declined, in no uncertain terms.)

But despite his celebrity, Spurgeon felt a deep connection with orphans, particularly those in his hometown of London. He regarded them as his children; he referred to them as "my orphans" and was committed to helping them.

In 1867 he established the Stockwell Orphanage, which provided food, shelter, clothing, and education to hundreds of London's orphans. The cigar-puffing young Spurgeon didn't revel in being a well-known public figure, but he decided that, as long as he was famous, he would put that fame to good use. He organized a massive annual "camp meeting," which drew vast crowds to hear one of the classic Spurgeon sermons.

He took a special offering at each meeting, and the events became a primary source of funding for the Stockwell Orphanage, which steadily grew to the point where it was caring for more than five hundred children.

At face value, it would be hard to find fault with a man like Spurgeon, but he did face criticism. Some thought he was too caught up in his own fame. Some considered the cigars unbecoming for a man of the cloth. Others were suspicious of the money a Spurgeon offering could command.

After the orphanage offering had been collected one year, a man tracked Spurgeon down. "Why, Mr. Spurgeon," the man accused, "I had always heard you preached for souls, not for money."

Spurgeon looked his accuser in the eye. "Sir," he said, "usually I do preach for souls, but my orphans cannot eat souls. And if they could, it would take four souls the size of yours to make a square meal for just one orphan!"

Not surprisingly, few, if any, critics dared to take Spurgeon to task after hearing of this encounter.

The Stockwell Orphanage continued to provide care to Spurgeon's orphan children, even after his death at the relatively young age of fifty-seven. During World War II, the orphanage was bombed out during the attacks on London. But after the war ended, Stockwell was rebuilt.

Today, Stockwell continues on. But it has a new name and a

broader focus. Called simply Spurgeons, the effort begun by a young preacher has grown into an international charity, serving children and families throughout the United Kingdom, as well as in Africa and Eastern Europe. Charles Spurgeon, no doubt, approves.

When a believing person prays,
great things happen.

—JAMES 5:16 NCV

PRAYER
AND LIGHTNING

ON A MUGGY SATURDAY AFTERNOON IN AUGUST 1806, five Williams College students gathered in a maple grove of Williamston, Massachusetts. They'd been meeting twice a week like this to pray. On this particular afternoon, however, winds gusted and lightning tore across the sky as they began to open their hearts to God. They took refuge from the storm in the shadow of a great haystack. One of their classes that day had centered on a discussion of China and India. One of the students, a freshman named Samuel Mills, said he felt they should pray that Christianity be sent to the Far East. The others agreed with him. In the midst of thunderclaps and roaring wind, they bowed their heads to quietly pray that God would touch the Far East.

The significance of that day would not be known for several more years.

By 1808 these same five, with India and China still on their hearts, formed the first college missionary society in the United States. They convinced the Association of Congregational Ministers of Massachusetts to form the first U.S. international missionary society, and in 1812 they sent five couples overseas as the first American missionaries to India. These were the first missionaries ever to leave the United States to live and minister in a foreign country.

Over the course of the next fifty years, the quintet saw another 1,250 missionaries sent to the Orient. These missionaries built missions and hospitals all across the Far East and translated the Bible into hundreds of languages, many for the first time. That meeting of five college students in the maple grove in 1806 became known as the Haystack Prayer Meeting, and scholars today view it as the beginning of American overseas missions.

But that was not all. Following the "Williams Five" example, students at several other American college campuses agreed to establish an annual day of prayer and fasting on the last Thursday of each February. They called it the "Concerts of Prayer." By 1826 these meetings became monthly. According to Henry C. Fish's *Handbook of Revivals*:

> In the year 1823 . . . the last Thursday of February in each year was agreed upon 'as the day for special supplication that God would pour from on high his Spirit upon our Colleges and Seminaries of learning.' And what have been some of the results? In the years 1824 and 1825 revivals were experienced in five different Colleges; in 1826 in six Colleges; in 1831 in nineteen. . . . In one of the Colleges it is stated that a revival started on the very day of the Concert. In 1835, not less than eighteen revivals were reported by different Colleges.

Those attending these events were asked to pray for three things:

(1) First, for themselves, that their character and wisdom would make them stand out as disciples of Jesus Christ—in the classroom and on the campus at large.

(2) Second, they prayed for the success of their colleges and

universities in fulfilling the reasons they had been created—most of which were formed to educate and equip ministers for spreading the ways of Jesus.

(3) Third, they prayed that God would pour out His Holy Spirit on college and university campuses; that students everywhere would realize their need for God, dedicate their lives to following Christ, and become representatives of the cross and the transformation it stands for.

During the United States' first one hundred years as a nation, college campuses were hotbeds of prayer. Things have certainly changed in the collegiate world. However, in February 2010—after a period of dormancy—the "Concerts of Prayer" event was revived as the Collegiate Day of Prayer on college campuses all across the United States. Who knows what amazing results might spring from this renewed commitment to prayer?

You don't have the things you want, because
you don't pray for them.

—JAMES 4:2 GWT

PRAYERS THAT CHANGED THE FATE OF NATIONS

THE MOST FAMOUS PRAYER VIGIL OF ALL TIME—one that lasted more than one hundred years—was started by a ragtag group of refugees who fled religious persecution in Moravia (now the Czech Republic) on May 27, 1722. Led by a young man named Christian David, the group consisted of three families who sought refuge at the Saxony estate of a rich twenty-one-year-old count named Nikolaus Ludwig von Zinzendorf.

When Christian had heard the plight of those in Moravia, he went to the count because of his reputation as a man of faith. Count Zinzendorf promised the refugees sanctuary on his vast estate in the town of Bethelsdorf. The families, however, decided to take up residence just outside of Bethelsdorf on a nearby hilltop the locals called "hutberg," or "watch hill," which was also on the count's estate and under his jurisdiction. Their desire was not to burden those in the township, but to support themselves and build their own "city on a hill." The village that emerged became known as Herrnhut (or "The Lord's Watch"), and in the years to come, Herrnhut became a refuge for anyone seeking religious freedom. The village's leaders, working together with the count in setting up initial ordinances and naming him as the local "governor" of sorts, strived to govern it according to the principles of the Bible.

According to the Old Testament book of 1 Samuel, when David fled persecution at the hands of King Saul, "Then everyone who was in trouble, in debt, or bitter about life joined him" (1 Samuel 22:2 GWT). The same thing happened to those living in Herrnhut. Many who had been kicked out of a church or been persecuted for their faith showed up on Christian David's doorstep.

Unfortunately, some of the refugees were no more than trouble-makers. These "wolves in sheep's clothing" began to take advantage of the sincerity and innocence of the other believers. They used their questionable interpretations of Scripture to control and manipulate their fellow villagers, creating division and strife among those in both the Herrnhut community and the larger town of Bethelsdorf.

Thus, what started as a group of earnest Christians seeking free-dom of worship soon turned into a band of backbiting, argumenta-tive malcontents. Neighbors fought over petty differences in their religious viewpoints. Some turned on Count Zinzendorf and the pastor in Bethelsdorf, Johann Rothe, calling them the "Beast of the Apocalypse and his False Prophet." Things grew so bad that Chris-tian David himself fell into being suspicious of and condescending toward everyone else to the point that he built himself a new home some distance away from the village—to keep himself from being "contaminated by the errors" of the others.

The Moravians were falling into the same pride and self-righteousness they had only recently fled from themselves. But God would not leave them to their own shortcomings.

Count Zinzendorf, for one, kept things in perspective, despite the name-calling and strife. Though young, he was not impetuous. Though rich and influential throughout all of Europe, he was determined to follow Jesus' teachings, no matter what it cost him. He wanted to expand the kingdom of God, not his own authority. Internationally, he used his influence with kings and nobility to bring them to Christ and spread God's love and truth. On his own properties, his theory of leadership was simple: "A man ought to look to God himself, in order to see how he governs the world, and learn from him how to govern, whether he have little or much to superintend."

Thus, amid the strife, his desire was not to repair his own reputation, but to restore the congregation at Herrnhut to its original purpose. He approached the villagers as servant, a friend in their time of need, though he was still their "landlord" and held authority over the village according to its original charter of governance.

So on May 12, 1727, the count used his authority to call for a general assembly of the villagers of Herrnhut, and in a convincing yet humble sermon, he brought the entire congregation to its knees in repentance for their divisiveness. They saw that their in-fighting had rendered them ineffective in fulfilling the dreams God had originally put into their hearts for their community. Neighbor reconciled with neighbor, and suddenly those who hadn't been able to pass in the street without bickering were meeting regularly to share meals and pray together. The summer of 1727 became known as the Golden

Summer among the Moravians, as the spirit of family replaced the spirit of suspicion and conceit. People gathered nightly on a hilltop to fellowship, sing hymns, and pray beneath a canopy of stars.

Three months later, the villagers shared a communion service with the congregation at Bethelsdorf. Zinzendorf described the event as "a day of the outpourings of the Holy Spirit . . . ; it was its Pentecost." As a result of the service, twenty-four men and twenty-four women agreed to begin a round-the-clock prayer vigil to call upon God to spread His kingdom on the earth. They each took an appointed one-hour shift during which they would pray seven days a week. Little did they know at the time that their vigil would continue on into the coming generations, spanning more than one hundred years.

On the heels of the vigil, the "Great Awakening" swept through England and the American colonies—a great missionary outpouring that sent Moravians all around the world. The awakening also saw the birth of evangelicalism, in the work of the Wesleys and George Whitefield; incredible manifestations of the Holy Spirit in the frontier revivals in Kentucky and Tennessee at the turn of the nineteenth century; and the beginning of the Second Great Awakening as Charles Finney began preaching in 1824.

PRAYER ITSELF IS AN ART WHICH ONLY THE HOLY SPIRIT CAN

TEACH US. PRAY FOR PRAYER. PRAY UNTIL YOU CAN REALLY PRAY.

—CHARLES H. SPURGEON

A ONE-WAY
TICKET

DEEPLY IMPRESSED IN HIS HEART that God wanted him to go to Mumbai, India, K. K. Devaraj bought one-way tickets for his wife, their four-year-old son, and himself in 1990. Since then he has been on a journey of following God that has led from one faith adventure to another.

Arriving in Mumbai, Devaraj had no plan other than to follow his heart, and it didn't take long for him to find something to lose his heart to. Mumbai's active and prolific red-light district regularly enslaved women and young children into prostitution. The streets seemed to be teeming with children—many of them children of prostitutes who saw little hope beyond growing up to be part of the brothels themselves.

In the meetings Devaraj held, the message from children they met was clear: "Take us out of this hell." Devaraj had no real resources or means of doing anything for these children, but as more children came to him, he knew he had one reliable resource: prayer. "Pray," he told them. "Pray and God will help us."

As they prayed one evening, Devaraj opened his eyes to see how the children were praying. He saw two who just knelt, heads down, weeping. The sight tore at Devaraj's heart. Within him he heard

God say, "I will answer their prayers and I will not let their tears fall just like that." Devaraj knew he had to be part of the answer to that prayer. He would take these children in as his own family. Delivering *his* children from the horrors of growing up in the red-light district became Devaraj's passion.

Devaraj was not a likely Christian. Growing up Hindu in India, he was well educated, and in the late 1970s he went to Iran to pursue a lucrative career in the oil industry. One day a friend brought him to a Bible study, where Devaraj experienced something he had never experienced before—a love that was beyond the natural. He knew it had to come from the one true God. Over the weeks of attending the study, Devaraj gave his heart to Jesus.

It was a bad time to be in Iran, though. In 1979 the Iranian revolution broke out, and Devaraj fled to Lebanon, which experienced a civil war of its own in the mid-1980s. Devaraj left for India in 1986, giving up his job and going to Bible school to prepare for the ministry. This led to the conviction in 1990 to go to Mumbai, where Devaraj and his family have lived ever since.

The work in Mumbai began small. First they rented a room to serve as a day care, a place to get the children off the streets for a few hours at a time. Then they established a shelter where the children could live while their mothers "worked." Soon Devaraj's team was making sure the children were in school during the day, gaining the knowledge and skills that would take them out of their cycles of poverty and prostitution. By 1995 Devaraj had organized the purchase of their first property outside of downtown Mumbai.

In Badlapur, a suburb of Mumbai, they opened orphanages for the children whose mothers had died of AIDS and other causes.

In the coming years the ministry grew quickly. Young men and women saved in the initial years would go to Bible school, then come back to join Devaraj's ministry team. The team saw miracle after miracle—whether it was finding a good price on a new building for outreach, seeing someone delivered from an addiction, or witnessing a healing.

One such story is that of Shabhanna and her younger brother, Pir. One day Devaraj was visiting a government hospital, and he heard a very young voice singing. He followed the sound to find a three-and-a-half-year-old girl singing to her one-and-a-half-year-old brother. The song was obviously her own. She sang, "Son, don't cry. Mommy died. I am your sister. I will go and beg money for you and educate you and make you a big boy."

After talking with the girl and the doctors, Devaraj eventually learned Shabhanna's story. Their mother was a prostitute who had become sick—probably from the HIV virus. She had three children: Pir, Shabhanna, and their older brother. When their mother became so sick no one wanted her anymore, she and her children were thrown out into the street. Shabhanna and her brothers sat with their mother in the streets, where she grew more and more ill and eventually died. Young Pir was also growing weaker, and when it looked as if he was near death, the older brother took him and Shabhanna to the hospital and then disappeared.

Doctors held little hope for Pir, who had tested positive for the

HIV virus, so they released him to one of the orphanages Devaraj had opened. But Shabhanna was sent to a state girls' home. Miraculously, under the orphanage's care, Pir grew stronger. Hoping to reunite the brother and sister, Devaraj and his team began petitioning the state for the right to take Shabhanna in as well. When the case came to trial, the judge didn't believe the young boy would remember his sister, so he asked that they meet before he made a decision. Pir was brought to the girls' home, and as the two saw each other, they ran to each other and embraced. Seeing this, the judge allowed Devaraj to take Shabhanna into their orphanage.

As of this writing, Shabhanna is about nine years old and Pir is about five—and both are doing well. In the orphanage, Shabhanna now not only cares for Pir but has taken many of the other young children under her wings, telling them they will all grow up to be strong and healthy in the power of Jesus.

Today, Devaraj's ministry, Bombay Teen Challenge (Mumbai was formerly known as Bombay), cares for almost three hundred children in their orphanages, day cares, and shelters. In downtown Mumbai they run a drug and alcohol rehabilitation center for young men and boys as well as an outreach that helps women escape prostitution. A church in the heart of the red-light district ministers to brothel owners, prostitutes, children, and patrons alike, seeing many come to Jesus and change their lives. Devaraj has also launched the Stop Sexual Slavery movement in India and around the world.

Despite all of this, Devaraj still has a holy discontent in his heart for the conditions of those in the red-light district of Mumbai. So Bombay Teen Challenge continues to grow, hoping to one day put the devil out of business in downtown Mumbai—to see families whole again and find children playing instead of begging for their next meal. Devaraj must, after all, take care of the sons and daughters to whom God gave Devaraj's heart.

"Go where the roads leave the city.
Invite everyone you find to the wedding."
The servants went into the streets and brought in all
the good people and all the evil people they found.
And the wedding hall was filled with guests.

—MATTHEW 22:9–10 GWT

FROM SMALL
BEGINNINGS

IN SEPTEMBER OF 1857, FOUR FRIENDS—James McQuilkin, Jeremiah "Jerry" Meneely, Robert Carlisle, and John Wallace—gathered in an old schoolhouse in Kells, Northern Ireland (called the province of Ulster at the time), to pray and study the Bible together. They met every Friday night, often bringing armfuls of peat with them to burn in the schoolhouse stove to keep them warm.

The four had much to pray for. At the time, Northern Ireland was plagued by alcoholism, public drunkenness, and the kind of crime spawned by the easy availability of hard liquor—combined with a poor economy and the harsh working conditions of an increasingly industrial nation.

In addition, the infamous potato famine left more than a million starved to death in the previous decade. A million more Irish citizens fled their country for a better life. Life expectancy for Irishmen averaged just forty years. To make matters even worse, the tension and violence between Irish Catholics and Protestants was spiking, making the island country a powder keg on the edge of civil war.

McQuilkin, Meneely, Carlisle, and Wallace knew that their land needed God's love, but what form would that love take? And what could four men do to help an entire country in peril? Still, while many of their countrymen and women spent their Fridays drinking and carousing, the foursome were faithful to band together and seek God for answers, even as fall gave way to a cold winter.

The foursome prayed and questioned one another about various Bible passages. They studied biographies of other Christian workers of their time to look for their insights. While the peat burned in the stove, a fire kindled inside of them, a fire to see change in their community and nation. For months, however, they saw no visible sign that their prayers were working.

Then, on New Year's Day of 1858, a new member joined the group, a young man they had been fervently praying for. Over the next few months, others joined the Friday night gatherings. By the end of the year, the weekly prayer group had grown to fifty, just enough to catch the attention of local ministers and their congregations.

But not all attention is welcome. Rather than supporting the schoolhouse prayer meetings, area churches branded its young members as arrogant, rebellious upstarts who didn't know their proper place in the local religious hierarchy. Ministers warned that the schoolhouse prayers wouldn't amount to anything because the group didn't understand the Bible well enough to pray correctly or effectively.

But the pray-ers kept coming.

As the schoolhouse group grew steadily, other small groups began prayer meetings of their own, emulating what was happening in Kells. More than one hundred barns, schoolrooms, business places, and private homes were hosting their own prayer sessions.

As more groups dotted the countryside, church services in the area began to see attendance swell. At some churches, people had to stand in doorways or listen at windows, as there was no room inside the building.

Soon, the prayer meetings outgrew the confines of available buildings. People gathered in fields and town squares throughout Northern Ireland. The town of Londonderry hosted several meetings a day, with as many as five thousand taking part.

In Coleraine, longtime denominational tensions were washed aside by a flood of people turning to God. It didn't matter if you were Presbyterian, Baptist, Congregationalist, or whatever, ministers had to come together to deal with the overflow of people hungry to know more about God. In Belfast, street people, drunkards, prostitutes, and criminals stood side by side with shopkeepers, schoolteachers, and craftsmen as more than twenty-five thousand gathered to hear of God's truths.

In parts of Ireland where alcohol-fueled violence had made citizens afraid to walk the street, bars closed. Distilleries went out of business. Criminal courts convened, only to discover there were no cases to try. Crime rates plummeted.

In County Antrim, for example, the jail and the police station were empty except for the employees.

In the shipyards of Harland and Wolff, laborers were moved to such high standards of honesty that they began returning tools and other things they had stolen over the years. So many items were collected that the company had to build a new storage facility to hold them all.

The 1859 Boyne Celebration, an annual gathering of Protestants that always erupted in fighting and bloodshed against the Catholics, instead erupted in the singing of hymns and the forming of prayer circles. As one minister reported, "There is no party spirit; no Orange [pro-Protestant] parade; no beating of drums; no exclamations [of] 'to hell with the pope,' no wickedness towards the Roman Catholics."

Northern Ireland was being transformed by the love of God so dramatically that even the North Seas would not contain the enthusiasm. The revival spread into Scotland, Wales, and England as well. Fathers who once came home stumbling drunk now led family prayer meetings and read from the Bible. Denominational divisions melted as people were so hungry to know God better that they crowded into any church whose doors were open. Seeking God became the business of the day rather than partying and fighting.

This particular time of cultural change and reform was so significant that it continues to be recognized 150 years later. On November 4, 2008, in the halls of the Northern Irish Assembly, David Simpson made a motion to have the Ministry of Culture, Arts, and Leisure organize events throughout the year to acknowledge "the positive contribution made by the Revival to society; [and] recognise that the positive impact of the Revival is still felt today."

The motion was debated with comments such as David Mc-Narry's:

> By the end of 1860, the effects of the Ulster revival included: strong services; unprecedented numbers of communicants; abundant prayer meetings; an increase in family prayers; unmatched scripture reading; prosperous Sunday schools; converts remaining steadfast; increased giving; the abatement of vice; and a reduction in crime. Such effects would be welcome if a revival happened in our country today.
>
> It is estimated that one million people were converted in the United Kingdom from the beginning of the revival in Kells. Missionaries carried the movement abroad and—fortunately—the consequences of the revival are still felt today and contribute significantly to various recognizable national characteristics that we protect.

The motion was passed with overwhelming support.

> Some people view religion as divisive and claim that it is the source of all the world's conflicts. It is the depravity of man's heart that causes today's conflicts. The 1859 revival demonstrated true biblical Christianity at its best and, as a result, people's lives changed. Today, we seek a society that is free of violence and the ills that are mentioned in the Chamber. . . . It is impossible to achieve those outcomes without seriously considering the impact of the 1859 revival, during which the gospel was preached. That gospel is not for unionism at the expense of nationalism, or vice versa—it is for everyone.
>
> **—MERVYN STOREY**, *member of the Legislative Assembly of Northern Ireland*

THE CLAPHAM
CONSPIRACY

IN 1792, WHEN WILLIAM WILBERFORCE MOVED into his friend Henry Thornton's London home on Clapham Common, little did he suspect that he would find more there than an easier commute to his work in the British Parliament.

The home was called Battersea Rise in a time when the homes and manors of the wealthy had names rather than street numbers. Though both Thornton and Wilberforce were men of considerable means—inherited wealth that would have let them sit back and enjoy comfortable lives of leisure all of their days—they chose instead to do the impossible.

In the grips of the emerging industrial revolution, London was described at the time as "one vast casino." As a rule, the rich—much of their wealth made from the labor of slaves conveniently out of sight on plantations in the West Indies—were absorbed in their card games and wooing one another's wives. Duels of honor for the smallest slight were commonplace. The poor, even children, were locked into eighteen-hour-a-day jobs in cotton mills or coal mines. What few shillings were scraped from this labor were often lost to the gin distillers so parents could try to drink away the wretchedness of their lives. Dank, dirty prisons overflowed with highwaymen, debtors, rapists, murderers, and petty thieves.

It wasn't uncommon to see a notorious robber and a child who stole a loaf of bread hung side by side as punishment for their crimes. Corruption ran from the streets all the way to the halls of government, where seats of authority were often purchased as easily as commodities on the local exchange.

Into this world came diminutive William Wilberforce. Standing barely five feet tall, he spoke like a lion and carried the conviction that "God Almighty has set before me two great objects, the suppression of the slave trade and the reformation of manners [moral values]." Writer James Boswell said of the first time he heard Wilberforce speak, "I saw what seemed a mere shrimp mount upon the table, but as I listened the shrimp grew and grew and became a whale."

Wilberforce was not alone in his quest for social transformation. In the five years he lived there, Battersea Rise became a gathering point for all who shared Wilberforce's and Thornton's God-given convictions. The house retained its purpose even after Wilberforce moved to a smaller house when he got married.

As their movement of social change grew, Thornton added thirty-four bedrooms to Battersea Rise to house the many visitors coming to help in their work. Some stayed for days, others lived there for years. The addition of a large, airy library, designed by Prime Minister William Pitt, made gatherings more comfortable. That library saw many fervent prayer meetings and debates that went on late into the night. The room also served as a place to conduct and store research. Some dedicated workers spent as many as ten hours a day scanning books, records, and whatever other evidence they found to aid their causes.

Zachary Macaulay became such a useful "tome" of information through this work that whenever Wilberforce needed information he would say, "Let's look it up in Macaulay." Those who sided with Wilberforce and Thornton in their voting for social improvement became negatively known as the Clapham Saints.

These "saints"—neighbors, fellow church members, and other sympathizers—from around the country gathered in Clapham to pray, plan, and collaborate about common practices that they saw as unjust and exploitive, from child labor standards to the slave trade. They collected information and artifacts from all over: thumb screws, manacles, branding irons, and whips. They discovered ship manifests that showed the tragic and sizable loss of life on slave ships from Africa—as many as half the slaves died before they made port. Testimonies from sailors about this cruelty turned the stomachs of even the staunchest supporters of slavery. They provided hard evidence of the barbarity of the slaving industry. None in the government assemblies could deny it.

However, despite all the work invested, those initial appeals met with defeat. Wilberforce's bills calling for the abolishment of slavery were defeated in 1788, 1789, 1790, 1791—and almost every year for the rest of the 1790s and into the 1800s. In 1804, a Wilberforce bill passed the House of Commons, but it was stalled until it was too late to be considered by the House of Lords.

In 1805 Wilberforce and his colleagues changed tactics slightly. They proposed a bill to ban British subjects from aiding or participating in the slave trade supplying French colonies. The measure passed, and the Clapham group continued their pressure until 1807, when slavery was finally abolished in the British Isles. Any slave that set foot there thereafter would be instantly set free.

The fight was not over, however. It would take until 1833 for slavery to be outlawed throughout the British Empire. The vote took place just weeks before Wilberforce's death.

For all of their lives, those at Clapham "conspired" to make the world a better place. While abolishing slavery in the British Commonwealth may have been the pinnacle of their success, it was far from their only endeavor. Members of the Clapham group were integral founders of the Church Missionary Society, which sent missionaries to Africa, India, Ceylon, China, Japan, Palestine, and Persia. They also founded the Religious Tract Society and the British and Foreign Bible Society. Some in the group became key directors of the Sierra Leone Company, which sought to free and repatriate African slaves to their native continent. They also organized a Society for the Bettering of the Condition of the Poor, one for the Relief of Debtors, and another for the Education of Africans, as well as championing other causes to help those in need or disadvantaged by social indifference throughout the British Empire.

In 1829 Francis Place, who was no friend to the Clapham group or their form of Christianity, wrote:

I am certain I risk nothing when I assert that more good has been done to the people in the last thirty years than in the three preceding centuries; that during this period they have become wiser, better, more frugal, more honest, more respectable, more virtuous than they ever were before.

Blessed are they who maintain justice,

who constantly do what is right.

—PSALM 106:3 NLT

Learn to do good. Work for justice.

Help the down-and-out. Stand up for the homeless.

Go to bat for the defenseless.

—ISAIAH 1:17 MSG

THE LORD'S PRAYER

This prayer has brought unity in the face of division for over two thousand years. It is next to impossible to humbly pray this prayer and come away feeling strife, anger, or hatred toward anyone.

When you pray, don't be like the hypocrites who love to pray publicly on street corners and in the synagogues where everyone can see them. I tell you the truth, that is all the reward they will ever get. But when you pray, go away by yourself, shut the door behind you, and pray to your Father in private. Then your Father, who sees everything, will reward you.

When you pray, don't babble on and on as people of other religions do. They think their prayers are answered merely by repeating their words again and again. Don't be like them, for your Father knows exactly what you need even before you ask him! Pray like this:

OUR FATHER IN HEAVEN,
    MAY YOUR NAME BE KEPT HOLY.
MAY YOUR KINGDOM COME SOON.
MAY YOUR WILL BE DONE ON EARTH, AS IT
    IS IN HEAVEN.
GIVE US TODAY THE FOOD WE NEED,
AND FORGIVE US OUR SINS,
    AS WE HAVE FORGIVEN THOSE WHO
SIN AGAINST US.
AND DON'T LET US YIELD TO TEMPTATION,
    BUT RESCUE US FROM THE EVIL ONE."

—MATTHEW 6:5–13 NLT

"AN APPOINTMENT
WITH GOD"

Hope Missionary Church in Bluffton, Indiana, started praying around the clock on March 5, 2006—and they have continued praying more than four years straight at this point. A few months into their season of day-and-night prayer, extraordinary things began to happen with some university students in the area. This story—written in first person by a young man who experienced a remarkable transformation and witnessed it in many others—highlights the main reason Jesus prayed that we would be one, so that the world would believe in Him. The names have been changed to protect the privacy of those involved.

IN AUGUST I WAS HANGING OUT with my friend Aimee when she told me she had to leave for her "appointment with God." Something inside me was curious, so when she invited me to come along, I did. During our hour in the prayer room, I accepted Christ. I cannot tell you how life-changing the experience has been for me, especially when I returned to my frat house and had to take my new friend Jesus with me.

Since that day, I have returned to the prayer room a few times—the prayer room at this church has continued day and night for over one year now. God has truly shown himself to me in huge and marvelous ways! I grew up with an abusive father, and I believed that I could never experience the love of a father. God has shown me differently. I have felt so loved and now experience peace every day, knowing that my heavenly Father is with me. I didn't ever think this was something I could feel!

During one of my visits to the prayer room, I saw a card on the wall, asking people to pray for the lost. It was humbling for me to read that, because I realized people I didn't know had been praying for me.

And, while in the prayer room, I couldn't get my frat brothers off my mind. Aimee explained that since I was now a disciple of Jesus, I had been called to seek others out and tell them of the great love I was experiencing. She prayed that I would have boldness and courage while doing this at school. She quoted Joshua 1:9: "Be strong and of good courage; do not be afraid, nor be dismayed, for the Lord your God is with you wherever you go" (NKJV).

I repeated this over and over in my head in the upcoming months. At school, I began to pray that all thirty-three of my frat brothers would give their lives to Christ. And one by one, they did! It was crazy—every couple days another guy would come to me and ask me to pray with him or tell me that he had already prayed to accept Christ as Savior and Lord. Praise God. How exciting it was for me to watch the transformation in my frat house. It was once a place about everything that didn't honor God, but now we were singing worship songs in our living room. God took over our house, and there was no turning back. When we left for Christmas break, everyone except a guy named Tim had become a Christian.

During break, Aimee was house-sitting and invited Tim over for dinner. By the end of the night he placed his faith in Christ as his Savior. Thirty-four frat brothers in less than six months! What a mighty God.

Little did we know how perfect God's timing was in all of this. Twenty-seven days after Tim placed his faith in Christ, he was involved in a fatal automobile accident and went to be with Jesus. Before he died, he had been consumed with the idea that his parents did not believe in Christ. At Tim's funeral, anyone who did not know Christ was invited to put their hope in the God that Tim loved. At his funeral, Tim's parents and fifteen of his high school football teammates decided to trust Christ and follow Him.

I believe all of this happened because there were people in that prayer room praying for the lost. I praise God for the church and their faithful obedience to God demonstrated through prayer. Thank you for praying for all of us.

> TALKING TO MEN FOR GOD IS A GREAT THING,
>
> BUT TALKING TO GOD FOR MEN IS GREATER STILL.
>
> —E. M. BOUNDS

> GOD IS NOT FINISHED WITH US BY A LONG SHOT. AS I ENTERED
> THE PRAYER ROOM TODAY, I WAS REMINDED AGAIN THAT THIS IS
> REALLY ABOUT HIM. HE HAS CALLED US TO KEEP PRAYING.
>
> —AN ANONYMOUS ENTRY ON THE
> HOPE MISSIONARY CHURCH PRAYER ROOM BLOG

A MIRACLE
ON FULTON
STREET

AT NOON ON SEPTEMBER 23, 1857, Jeremiah Lanphier sat alone in a room. He removed from his Bible the copy of the handbill and read again the words he had written:

> A day Prayer Meeting is held every Wednesday, from 12 to 1 o'clock, in the Consistory building in the rear of the North Dutch Church, corner of Fulton and William Streets (entrance from Fulton and Ann Streets).
>
> This meeting is intended to give merchants, mechanics, clerks, strangers, and businessmen generally an opportunity to stop and call upon God amid the perplexities incident to their respective avocations. It will continue for one hour; but it is also designed for those who may find it inconvenient to remain more than five or ten minutes, as well as for those who can spare the whole hour.

Hearing a noise, Jeremiah looked up at the door. No one was there. He pulled out his pocket watch to look at the time: 12:07 p.m. Chairs were strewn everywhere in anticipation of a decent crowd, but they were all empty—no one had showed up. He refolded the flyer, placed it back in his Bible, and set both on a table beside him. He walked over to the large map of the world that took up most of the wall in front of the room. He pondered it for a moment, then returned to his seat. He bowed his head to pray alone.

Jeremiah had handed out and posted the flyers all over downtown New York City. As it was already his practice to stop his work and pray during the noon hour—and as he had noticed so many other workers in that area out on the street eating lunch or idle at that hour of the day—he thought he would invite others to join him. *Who knows?* he thought. *Next week might be different.*

Only a few months earlier, he had left his business to accept appointment as a city missionary for downtown New York City. He'd found Jesus in a meeting preached by Charles Finney at the Broadway Tabernacle many years earlier, and now he wanted to devote his life to expanding God's kingdom.

Jeremiah looked at his watch again. It was now 12:22 p.m. He looked longingly at the door. Still no one came.

New York certainly needed prayer. Times were tough. The California gold rush had spawned speculative businesses all over the East Coast, including New York. Many of these businesses were run fast and loose, and it was easy for executives to pocket much of the profit, rather than reinvest it or set it aside as security. When several factors hit at once, including British financiers pulling their money from American holdings, the economy collapsed. The fact that fifteen tons of gold had just been lost at sea in transit from San Francisco to New York had not helped matters either. Banks were forced to close, factories laid off entire workforces, goods piled up in warehouses because no one was buying them, and several railways declared bankruptcy.

Thousands of merchants closed their shops as a result, and roughly thirty thousand men in New York City found themselves looking for work.

These woes must have weighed heavily on Jeremiah's mind as he continued to pray on that September day. At half past the noon hour, he looked up from his prayers, hearing footsteps on the stairs outside of the room. As he watched, a man ascended the stairs and appeared in the doorway. "Is this where the prayer meeting is?" he asked. Jeremiah nodded and crossed the room to introduce himself. As he did, another man arrived. Another followed. He greeted each warmly.

When the number reached six, he moved to the circle of chairs he had set out for the gathering, and organized them into a smaller circle. Then he welcomed everyone again. "Brothers, I am glad you could make it," he said. "Since it is what we have come here to do, let us pray. Our Father in heaven . . ." As Jeremiah prayed, the others bowed their heads to join him.

The next Wednesday, twenty people showed up. The Wednesday after that, the number doubled. The next Wednesday, the group decided to meet daily instead of weekly. Similar gatherings began popping up elsewhere in New York. By the beginning of 1858, Jeremiah's prayer meeting was so crowded that it expanded to rooms on three separate floors.

By March he moved his group into a theater. He had no choice.

More than six thousand people attended regularly. Meanwhile, business lunch prayer meetings began sprouting up as far away as Pittsburgh and at five well-known locations in Washington, D.C. It was soon quite common for people shopping during the noon hour to see store signs that read "We will re-open at the close of the prayer meeting."

By October 1858, ten thousand were gathering daily for prayer in the various locations. New England was being reborn. It was a quiet revival that took place without many preachers or big names attached to it. People were simply finding Jesus and becoming inspired with a deep passion to pray for their friends and loved ones. Pastor Charles Finney wrote, "This winter of 1857–58 will be remembered as the time when a great revival prevailed. It swept across the land with such power that at the time it was estimated that not less than 50,000 conversions occurred weekly."

People curious about knowing the Jesus they were hearing so much about flocked to churches. There they found Him and wouldn't let go. Then they would go out and excitedly tell their friends about what they had found and bring them to church the next Sunday. Across New England, Jesus was commonly discussed on street corners, in shops, and wherever people gathered. Families prayed together every night, and people everywhere shared the amazing things God was doing in their lives. Because of where it had started—with seven men gathering in a room to pray—the movement became known as "The Fulton Street Revival." Others called it "The Prayer Meeting Revival." Through it, New England was transformed in roughly three years, and many of her citizens would go on to fight to end slavery and rejoin the union of the United States when the Civil War erupted in 1860.

It is interesting to note that Jeremiah Lanphier's prayer meeting in New York started the same month as that of the four friends—James McQuilkin, Jeremiah Meneely, Robert Carlisle, and John Wallace— in Northern Ireland. In fact, in 1858 ministers for Ireland came to New York to take part in Lanphier's prayer meetings to learn from them and take some of "the fire" back to Great Britain. But while these meetings started at the same time, they progressed in different ways. Only the common links of time, crossing denominational lines to pray together, and the resulting cultural change connected them.

Yes, it's true that God works in mysterious ways, but it is no mystery that He always moves in answer to heartfelt, unified prayer.

And day by day, attending the temple together and breaking bread in their homes, they received their food with glad and generous hearts, praising God and having favor with all the people. And the Lord added to their number day by day those who were being saved.

—ACTS 2:46–47 ESV

THE WHITE
ROSE

IN 1941 HANS SCHOLL WAS A conscripted soldier in Hitler's army. He had been assigned to spend a year as part of the occupational force in Poland and southern Russia. Here he saw Russians and Jews used as slave labor, something that twisted his insides. One day as he saw a young Jewish girl forced to dig ditches, his heart went out to her. The thought occurred to him, *There, but for the grace of God, I could have been—or one of my sisters.* He gave the young girl his rations, but she refused, suspicious of his kindness. So he pulled a flower from alongside the road and offered again. Seeing he meant nothing but kindness, she accepted. Soon he moved on and eventually returned to school as a medical student with some friends and his sister Sophie, who was studying to be a nurse. Every time he heard rumors of the concentration camps, he thought of that young girl and wondered what had become of her.

One day Sophie came to Hans, deeply troubled. She had read a sermon by the Bishop of Muenster, Clemens Galen, denouncing the Nazi Aryan Eugenics plans to "euthanize" mentally ill and developmentally disabled patients for the good of German "blood-lines." As a medical student, Sophie was mortified by the inhumanity and cold-bloodedness of this logic and its lack of compassion for the innocent. Galen preached that this program "was against God's commandments, against the law of nature, and against the system of jurisprudence in Germany." Shocked by her report, Hans and some other students made copies of the sermon and distributed them as pamphlets. Because distributing any publications not approved by the government was illegal, the students discreetly left piles of them in school hallways when no one was looking. Others they mailed to various private homes and public houses in typed envelopes.

As news of the war grew worse, Hans and Sophie felt compelled to speak out again. They and a trusted group of friends—Alexander Schmorell, Willi Graf, Jürgen Wittenstein, Christoph Probst, and one of their professors, Kurt Huber—banded together into what they called the Society of the White Rose. Their goal, inspired by both their faith and their disgust at the war's injustices, was to simply tell the truth—a truth that the official press obscured with propaganda. The group's publications called for a return to democracy in Germany, as well as for social justice for German, Jew, and foreigner alike.

Using phone books, the group found the addresses of college professors and other people of influence and began mailing leaflets to them. They also targeted random home addresses they saw in their daily life. And, of course, they continued to leave anonymous stacks of literature in the school's hallways between classes.

In order to broaden their influence, they traveled to different parts of the country on weekends to gather more names and addresses.

Then, in early 1943, came news of the Nazi defeat at Stalingrad, in which hundreds of thousands of Germans were killed in battle. Many of the dead were the age of Hans and Sophie; some were even younger. All told, more than two million died on both the Axis and Allied sides. More than ninety thousand Germans were taken captive, many of whom would die as prisoners of war.

News of this devastation convinced the members of the White Rose that it was time to call for the end of the war. On the nights of February 4, 8, and 15, they snuck into the silent streets of Munich to paint anti-Hitler slogans on walls. They wrote "Hitler the Mass Murderer!" "Down with Hitler!" and "Freedom! Freedom! Freedom!" They also painted huge crossed-out swastikas as symbols of their call for action.

In further hope of inspiring a youth uprising, they printed more leaflets than they ever had before. They published nine thousand despite the strict wartime rationing of ink and paper. They titled this leaflet, their sixth, *Fellow Fighters in the Resistance*. It began:

> Shaken and broken, our people behold the loss of the men of Stalingrad. Three hundred and thirty thousand German men have been senselessly and irresponsibly driven to death and destruction by the inspired strategy of our World War I Private First Class [referring to Hitler]. . . .
>
> The name of Germany is dishonored for all time if German youth do not finally rise, take revenge, smash its tormentors. Students! The German people look to us.

As soon as copies of this leaflet fell into the hands of the Gestapo, they activated all officers to find those who had any part in writing, printing, or distributing it. The students had been extremely careful not to be seen with the piles of pamphlets, but when Sophie, in a whimsical act of defiance, flung a handful off the third-floor balcony of the medical school, a witness reported her. In short order she was arrested. Once her identity was known, it didn't take long for the authorities to round up everyone she knew well and start questioning them.

Four days later, Sophie and the others found themselves on trial for treason. With little regard for due process, Hans, Sophie, and Christoph Probst were sentenced to execution by guillotine. The sentence was to be carried out that afternoon.

Sophie's last encounter with her parents was recorded in the book *A Noble Treason* by Richard Hanser:

Then a woman prison guard brought in Sophie.

She was wearing her everyday clothes, a rather bulky crocheted jacket and a blue skirt, and she was smiling. Her mother tentatively offered her some candy, which Hans had declined.

"Gladly," said Sophie, taking it. "After all, I haven't had any lunch!"

She, too, looked somehow smaller, as if drawn together, but her face was clear and her smile was fresh and unforced, with something in it that her parents read as triumph.

"Sophie, Sophie," her mother murmured, as if to herself. "To think you'll never be coming through the door again!" Sophie's smile was gentle.

"Ah, Mother," she said, "Those few little years . . ."

Sophie Scholl looked at her parents and was strong in her pride and certainty. "We took everything upon ourselves," she said. "What we did will cause waves."

Her mother spoke again: "Sophie," she said softly, "remember Jesus."

"Yes," replied Sophie earnestly, almost commandingly, "but you, too."

She left them, her parents, Robert and Magdalene Scholl, with her face still lit by the smile they loved so well and would never see again. She was perfectly composed as she was led away. Robert Mohr [the Gestapo official in charge of her initial questioning], who had come out to the prison on business of his own, saw her in her cell immediately afterwards, and she was crying.

It was the first time Mohr had seen her in tears, and she apologized. "I have just said good-bye to my parents," she said. "You understand . . ." She had not cried before her parents. For them she had smiled.

As Christoph Probst prepared to face his death, he received news that his wife had just given birth to their third child. She knew nothing about what was happening to him. After receiving his last rites from a priest, Christoph said, "Now my death will be easy and joyful."

Hans, Sophie, and Christoph died with dignity and honor within the next few hours. Having dared to "step across the line," they were looking more ahead to the glory they were about to experience in heaven than the evil they left behind. Just as the blade was about to fall across Hans's neck, he called out, "Long live freedom!" A single rose was later found in his pocket.

ONE DAY I WAS WALKING PAST THE
MEMORIAL IN FRANZ JOSEF STREET TO
SOPHIE SCHOLL, A YOUNG GIRL
WHO OPPOSED HITLER, AND I REALIZED
THAT SHE WAS THE SAME AGE AS ME
AND THAT SHE WAS
EXECUTED THE SAME YEAR
I STARTED WORKING FOR HITLER.
AT THAT MOMENT I REALLY SENSED
THAT IT WAS NO EXCUSE TO
BE YOUNG AND THAT IT MIGHT HAVE
BEEN POSSIBLE TO FIND OUT WHAT HAD
BEEN GOING ON.

—TRAUDL JUNGE, *one of Hitler's
private secretaries*

THE ONE-MINUTE REMIX

Over and over in life, we are faced with the choice to either add to the walls that separate people or to tear them down. Amazing things happen when people make choices to come together.

In Japan, an elderly man calmed and comforted a dangerous drunk by treating him like a son, not an enemy. In the 1800s, Charles Spurgeon looked at London's orphans as his own children and rescued hundreds of them from destitute lives. And he founded a ministry that continues on today.

Jeremiah Lanphier put out an open prayer-meeting invitation to his fellow New Yorkers. At first, it looked like he would be the sole attendee. But then people started to respond. And eventually Lanphier had more than ten thousand prayer partners.

Life bears out the lesson over and over: We are better together. But togetherness doesn't just happen. People choose to make it happen. Will you be one of those people?

A PRAYER
FOR CHOOSING
THE GOOD

This section's concluding prayer is from Saint Francis of Assisi, who—although he was from a wealthy family—gave up everything to serve God and others.

LORD, MAKE ME AN INSTRUMENT OF YOUR PEACE.

WHERE THERE IS HATRED, LET ME SOW LOVE;

WHERE THERE IS INJURY, PARDON;

WHERE THERE IS DOUBT, FAITH;

WHERE THERE IS DESPAIR, HOPE;

WHERE THERE IS DARKNESS, LIGHT;

AND WHERE THERE IS SADNESS, JOY.

O DIVINE MASTER, GRANT THAT I MAY NOT

   SO MUCH SEEK

TO BE CONSOLED AS TO CONSOLE;

TO BE UNDERSTOOD AS TO UNDERSTAND;

TO BE LOVED AS TO LOVE.

FOR IT IS IN GIVING THAT WE RECEIVE;

IT IS IN PARDONING THAT WE ARE PARDONED;

AND IT IS IN DYING THAT WE ARE BORN

   TO ETERNAL LIFE. AMEN.

If you gotta start somewhere
why not here?

SECTIONFOUR

If you gotta start sometime

why not now?

THROUGH THE FOG
THERE IS HOPE
IN THE DISTANCE

HOPE IS JUST A PRAYER AWAY

If you do not hope, you will not find what is beyond your hopes.

—**SAINT CLEMENT OF ALEXANDRIA**

Where two or three have come together in my name,
I am there among them. —**MATTHEW 18:20 GWT**

For he has said, "I will never leave you nor forsake you."

—**HEBREWS 13:5 ESV**

An old monk was asked, "What do you do here
in this monastery?" His reply: "We fall, we get up.
We fall, we get up. We fall, we get up."

YOU CAN DO MORE THAN PRAY, AFTER YOU HAVE PRAYED, BUT
YOU CANNOT DO MORE THAN PRAY UNTIL YOU HAVE PRAYED.
—JOHN BUNYAN

Surely I am with you always, to the very end of the age.
—MATTHEW 28:20 NIV

ALL DIFFICULTIES IN PRAYER CAN BE TRACED TO ONE CAUSE: PRAYING
AS IF GOD WERE ABSENT. —TERESA OF AVILA

The kingdom of God is within you. —LUKE 17:21 NKJV

TOBYMAC

JADED OR **JOYFUL?**

IF YOU WERE MAKING A RECORD WITH ME— whether you were singing backing vocals, playing rhythm guitar, or co-writing a song—there's one thing you'd need for sure.

Patience.

Anyone who has worked with me knows I can be relentless about making music.

I have been known to work day after day, tweaking and massaging every vocal nuance, every drum fill, every lyric. Whatever it takes to make a song sound just right.

The truth is, I have to work really hard at making music. I feel like I have to work harder than other people to get there musically and lyrically. That's what drives me. I usually don't sit down and write a great song in just a few minutes, like other artists can. But I think my work ethic makes up for that. I have to push myself to get beyond a song that's only "very good." To dig deep for something more.

I admit, however, that I have to fight really hard to remain unjaded—to keep believing that I can actually walk into my studio and write a song that breathes life. That's the hardest fight for a guy who's been doing this for a while. It could be easy to fall into the trap of just making music your job. When I write, I continually make it a point of asking God to hollow me of my junk and breathe something through me that is bigger than I am.

You might feel the same way about your gig, whatever it is. Whether

BLOG

you're a parent, a student, a teacher, a youth leader, or an artist of some kind, the routine of what you do can dim the passion. Especially when you've been at it awhile. Long enough to see some of your peers taking shortcuts or manipulating people and circumstances for selfish personal gain. Or people doing just enough to get by—but somehow enjoying more success than you.

One of my favorite Bible verses is Isaiah 43:19, which declares that God is "doing a new thing." That's the essence of being unjaded—believing that God is going to do something through a song that I write, a conversation I have, or a concert I perform. That hope has given me the enduring hope that has carried me through long, exhausting weeks on the road, away from my family. Through negative reviews in the media. Past the trap of becoming jaded. Through the inevitable artistic conflicts.

When we stay plugged into who God is—and keep our eyes searching for that hope through the fog—He can do amazing things through our efforts. One example is the story of one of my management associates, Philip Peters. Philip took a missions trip to Antigua as a teenager about twelve years ago. There, he met Gerald Lafleur, a Haitian-born college student training to be a pastor. Philip and Gerald struck up a friendship and pledged to keep in touch.

They did. Eight years after their first meeting, Philip flew to Haiti and worked with his friend, now Pastor Lafleur, to start a ministry called Restore Haiti (www.restorehaiti.com) in the city of Jacmel.

The ministry's name is especially poignant when you realize that "Restore Haiti" preceded the devastating 2010 earthquake by several years. This is a country long in need of restoration. It is the poorest nation in the entire Western Hemisphere. It provides no free public education to its children, so many of them are born into a prison of poverty, ignorance, and despair.

But Philip and Pastor Lafleur are doing their part to change things. Restore Haiti launched a child-sponsorship program, and already more than 120 Haitian children have been matched with sponsors. These sponsorships provide school tuition, school uniforms, textbooks, and a hot daily meal to desperately needy students.

To Philip and Pastor Lafleur, who love Haiti and its people, the 2010 earthquake was of course devastating on every possible level—physically, financially, emotionally, and spiritually. But all of the people behind Restore Haiti are fighting off discouragement. "I learn to get by on little victories," Philip says, noting that the building constructed to feed students is no longer adequate to hold them all. Meals have to be served in two shifts.

"There is so much to be done," Philip adds, "but I'm learning to trust God . . . that He will make this city whole again in His time."

As evidence that his trust is being rewarded, Philip points to an intriguing fact: As Jacmel and other Haitian cities are being restored, rubble recovered after the earthquake is a key building material.

In this section you'll see even more stories of how God is working through His people to bring hope to a world in desperate need of it.

It's important to remember that God can also do small, simple things that make people's lives a little bit better, if only for a few moments. Whatever we do in God's name, in His Spirit, always matters. Let's pray for each other, that we keep this truth in mind. That we avoid becoming jaded. That we find joy and meaning in our work.

INTO THE
JAWS OF HELL

JEANNINE BRABON IS ONE OF THE LAST PEOPLE you'd expect to find in the jaws of hell. Yet it's a place she spends much of her time.

Brabon is a serious academic, a professor at Seminario Biblico de Colombia (the Biblical Seminary of Colombia). She is a Hebrew scholar, specializing in biblical Hebrew and its interpretation. She translated the massive LaSor's Hebrew Grammar into Spanish.

But Brabon is also a missionary, and this calling flows from her work in the classroom. "I teach people who have had their fathers, brothers, and sons assassinated," she explains. "I rarely have a class in any given year in which a student doesn't lose a family member to a violent death. Life is of little value. It's a deadly and dangerous world. But security is not the absence of danger; it's the presence of Jesus."

One day, a girl named Margarita, one of Brabon's students, asked for help searching for her brother, who had been missing for five days. Their search led them to the morgue in the city of Medellin, home to the infamous drug cartel of the same name. In Medellin twenty-five deaths occur every day, with more than a hundred on a typical weekend.

At the morgue Brabon and Margarita searched through more than one hundred bodies.

Brabon says she will never forget Margarita's cries when she found her brother, who had been brutally tortured to death. As Brabon and her student cried together, a question exploded in the professor's mind: *What can I do? What can I do?*

Shortly after the experience in the morgue, Brabon was invited to speak at Bellavista Prison, which had earned the nickname "Jaws of Hell." In the mid-1970s, the prison was built to house fifteen hundred inmates. By the end of the 1980s, it swelled with more than sixty-six hundred dangerous criminals—drug lords, terrorists, assassins for hire.

Dead bodies, some of them decapitated, littered the prison floor. Walls were covered with graffiti, written in blood.

Prison riots were commonplace, and Bellavista averaged about forty-five murders a month. Often, the guards were so terrified that they refused to pass through the prison gates to report for work. The prison had become, essentially, a training ground for Medellin's killing fields. Once outside the prison walls, either through parole or escape, a Bellavista ex-con would likely join the ranks of the city's three thousand contract criminals, criminals who specialized in blackmail, kidnapping, and murder. Or one could join any of the more than 120 gangs, all ready to kill for pay. According to one Colombian newspaper, the country was averaging twenty-five thousand murders annually, and Medellin was a major source of the country's woes.

So, not surprisingly, the invitation from Bellavista left an unassuming female missionary/professor feeling inadequate. And terrified. But Brabon clung to a Scripture verse: "The wicked flee when no man pursueth: but the righteous are bold as a lion" (Proverbs 28:1 KJV).

Standing in front of her criminal audience, Professor Brabon preached about God's steadfast love. As she concluded, twenty-three crying men came forward to dedicate their lives to Jesus Christ.

That was only the beginning.

Brabon soon launched a Bible training school, the Bible Training Institute, within Bellavista's walls. She spends two days a week inside the prison, teaching inmates and witnessing to them about Jesus' life-transforming love. The Institute's rigorous two-year curriculum transforms inmates into spiritual leaders. The program is no joke. When an inmate graduates, the dean of Seminario Biblico de Colombia hands him the diploma.

More than forty inmates study at the Institute at a given time, and the total number of graduates is closing in on one thousand.

Brabon does more than teach in the Jaws of Hell. She meets with law enforcement officers, politicians, and prison officials to advocate for better conditions. (Such as basic sanitation for the prisoners.) She witnesses to prisoners and guards.

Not surprisingly, some in Medellin don't appreciate hit men, drug lords, and terrorists "going soft" and losing their value to the drug cartel. Thus, Brabon lives under the constant threat of death. Her movements are tracked by Medellin's criminal element, forcing her to regularly change her daily routines and travel routes.

Once, an inmate infiltrated one of Brabon's prayer groups and later made a false accusation about Brabon and a colleague—to a powerful guerrilla commander. The commander issued a death decree on both of them.

When he heard about the decree, however, the inmate panicked. Guilt-stricken, he rushed to Brabon and confessed what he had done. Then he informed the guerrilla commander that he had levied false charges, and the death threat was lifted. Brabon was matter-of-fact about the incident. "We are not to fear those who kill the body," she said. "We are to fear the sin that will destroy us eternally. Our greatest concern ought to be that we die to sin daily."

Meanwhile, despite the cloud of danger that is Brabon's constant companion, Bellavista Prison continues to experience what can only be called a revival. And God had begun working there even before Brabon arrived. At one crucial point in the prison's history, its riots threatened to spill over into the city. It appeared that the military would have to be called in. The media gathered, expecting to cover a massacre. However, instead of unleashing the Colombian army, the prison warden honored the request of a small group of Christians. They wanted to hold a prayer meeting—inside the prison walls.

While the riots raged, the small band of believers prayed fervently. Soon, prisoners began turning in their weapons—not to the guards but to a former inmate who was now a volunteer chaplain.

This chaplain had earned the prisoners' trust, reporting to his post at eight o'clock every morning for three years and ministering within Bellavista's walls—regardless of how bad prison conditions were on any given day. He showed up when the guards would not.

Brabon described the disaster averted in clear terms: "God is moving in unprecedented ways. The Holy Spirit is giving life where death reigns."

Today, those who have seen it describe Bellavista as "a model prison." A most unlikely beacon of hope in a land darkened by evil. More than 150 faithful inmates crowd into the prison chapel for daily services. Smaller groups meet twice daily on prison patios and pavilions. A daily radio broadcast offers counseling and helps inmates communicate their newfound faith to their families. During weekend visitations, inmates hold evangelistic services for their families and friends. Imprisoned men proclaim the freedom they have found in Jesus Christ.

In a recent thirteen-year period, Bellavista saw zero riots. And the murder rate dropped to less than one a year, a fraction of the forty-five monthly killings the prison once endured.

One telling sign of Bellavista's transformation occurred after the terrorist attacks of September 11, 2001. The Colombian prisoners committed themselves to praying for the United States—and all those affected by the tragedy. As a show of their ongoing prayer support, a few prisoners carved a pair of praying hands, which were eventually delivered to then-President George W. Bush. The president kept the carving in the Oval Office to remind him of the faithful prayers of a group of former drug lords, terrorists, and hit men.

What has transformed the Jaws of Hell? Perhaps it is fitting to give one of Bellavista's inmates the last word:

"God chose what is foolish in the world to shame the wise," says the convict. "God chose what is weak in the world to shame the strong. God chose what is low and despised in the world, so that no human being might boast in the presence of God."

I'll call nobodies and make them somebodies;
I'll call the unloved and make them beloved.
In the place where they yelled out, "You're nobody!"
they're calling you "God's living children."

—ROMANS 9:25–26 MSG

WHEN THE END
IS THE BEGINNING

ANDREA JAEGER WAS NOT YOUR TYPICAL MIDDLE-SCHOOLER.
While many of her classmates were experiencing their first crushes,
the fourteen-year-old Chicago native was crushing the world's best
tennis players. Displaying athleticism and a preternaturally powerful
forehand, she defeated legends like Chris Evert, Martina Navrati-
lova, Tracy Austin, and Billie Jean King. Not long after blowing out
the candles on her fifteenth birthday cake, she became the young-
est player ever to be seeded at Wimbledon. By the time she was
sixteen, she was ranked the number-two tennis player in the world.

Jaeger's prodigious ability—combined with her endearing braces
and blond pigtails—made her a media darling. But away from the
tennis spotlight, Andrea's life was miserable. Her classmates re-
sented her success—which isolated her from most of her peers.
In the lunchroom, students tossed food at her. In the hallways,
they threw her into lockers. "It wasn't a fun time to grow up," she
understates.

But the abuse didn't harden Jaeger's heart; it made her more
compassionate. At age fifteen, she was riding in a limo, returning
from a tennis match in New Jersey. When the car approached a

toy store, she asked the driver to stop. She dashed into the store and bought several hundred dollars' worth of toys, which she then delivered to children in the critical-care unit of New York's Helen Hayes Hospital. "I just felt a calling at that moment," she would explain later.

As her life on the pro tennis circuit continued, Jaeger continued to surprise hospitalized kids with visits and gifts purchased with her prize money. The compassion she held for children felt like a hunger that would never be satisfied.

But at only nineteen, with years of her best tennis ahead of her, Andrea Jaeger was aced by misfortune. She suffered a shoulder injury that would soon end her career.

She spent no time crying about it, however. She accepted that she could no longer be a tennis champion, so she committed her life to being a champion of children in need. She threw herself into creating a foundation for children with cancer. The one-time world-class athlete took a job as an airline ticket agent so that she could use the air miles she accrued to conduct research, raise funds, and visit sick children.

Jaeger spent years building infrastructure for her foundation. Several tennis players contributed to the cause. A married couple donated ten acres of land, and a businessman provided $1.7 million to build an eighteen-thousand-foot facility. For her part, Jaeger poured her tennis earnings, about $1.4 million, into the effort.

Finally, in her mid-twenties Jaeger launched the Silver Lining Foundation in Aspen, Colorado. Silver Lining's mission is simple:

to make life better for terminally ill kids. Every year, Silver Lining welcomes children from across the country. They receive counseling and emotional support. They get to escape the daunting challenges in their lives and lose themselves in the pure abandon of activities like horseback riding and white-water rafting.

As one of the foundation's volunteers describes it, Jaeger helps children "abandon being treated like a sick person. The children really bloom."

"Andrea does this for all the right reasons," says model/actress Cindy Crawford, a frequent Silver Lining volunteer. "It shines through her actions. She is utterly selfless and completely devoted to helping others."

Today, Jaeger divides her time between working directly with kids in Colorado and traveling the country to raise money toward her foundation's $2 million annual budget. She also underwrites reunions and retreats for families affected by cancer, provides college scholarships, and brings Silver Lining programs to children who are too sick to travel.

Additionally, she has launched two other humanitarian efforts. The Little Star Foundation expands on the mission of Silver Lining, assisting children affected by disease, neglect, and poverty. Little Star's first major benefactor was John McEnroe, tennis's notorious, tantrum-throwing "bad boy" during his playing days.

The other effort, Athletes for Hope, encourages sports stars to be more charitable people, to use their resources and influence for the good of humanity, especially the needy. Among those who have joined Jaeger in this cause are Andre Agassi, Lance Armstrong, Tony Hawk, and Muhammad Ali.

Those who interact with Jaeger these days refer to her as Sister Andrea. In 2006 she gave up all her material possessions and was ordained by the Episcopal Church as an Anglican Dominican nun.

A journey from teen tennis phenom to philanthropist/nun might seem bizarre, but Sister Andrea doesn't see it that way. "By giving me such a talent for the sport of tennis," she explains, "God gave me the chance to prepare for bigger challenges and purposes in my life."

Looking back on the career-ending injury, Jaeger is similarly philosophical. Even as a teen, she explains, she had her eyes and heart set on something more significant than tennis. "My family and friends were so upset when I got hurt," she recalls. "But I knew in my heart that I was called to help kids. Because of how I was treated when I was younger, I know this: Everyone can use someone who cares."

Make a careful exploration of who you are and the work you have been given, and then sink yourself into that. Don't be impressed with yourself. Don't compare yourself with others. Each of you must take responsibility for doing the creative best you can with your own life.

—GALATIANS 6:4–5 MSG

NEW HOPE ACADEMY:
A "CITY ON OUR KNEES"
GOES TO SCHOOL

IS A "CITY ON OUR KNEES" JUST A DREAM? Can a group of very diverse and very different individuals actually let down their guard, set aside their preconceptions, and become one people—growing together as they worship and pray to one God?

How could such a city be built—and how would it function?

Perhaps a small elementary school in Franklin, Tennessee, holds some answers.

In the early 1990s, Paige Pitts, a young twenty-something woman, was enlisted by her pastors at Christ Community Church to begin pounding the pavement in Franklin, focusing on the city's urban community. Her goal—to build relationships. Franklin, like many U.S. cities, is a dichotomy. It is home to thousands of families full of material wealth, many from the music and entertainment industries. Miley Cyrus attended high school in Franklin. Oprah Winfrey has a home on a hillside there.

Williamson, the county Franklin represents, is the twelfth wealthiest in the nation. But portions of the city, particularly those that are predominately African American, stand in stark contrast to the surrounding affluence. There are families that scrape to get by. Many children, because of their environment, enter the education system with significant disadvantages.

Not surprisingly, many of Paige's encounters were poignant. She talked with one young teen, asking him about his hopes for the future. He shared his dream of playing in the National Basketball Association.

Paige reminded him of the stark odds NBA hopefuls face. She asked him about a backup plan. Each backup plan was another sport. She pressed in: "What if sports are not an option?"

The question seemed to stymie the young man. After a while he shrugged. "I guess I'll just work at McDonald's."

Stories like this one impressed upon Paige the dire need for vision and for top-quality education in Franklin's under-served areas. With the help and prayers of her church's community-ministries organization—and the conviction that education is a key antidote to poverty and hopelessness—she began tutoring children in the afternoons. As she became more and more engaged in the children's lives, seeing firsthand some of the obstacles they faced, she began dreaming of a school.

She had a vision for a school that would transform students' lives, and the community at large, by shattering social-class barriers, fostering racial reconciliation, and sharing God's love.

The school became a focal point of prayer for Paige—and for area churches and ministries. In some cases, the various groups didn't even know about each other, even though they were praying for the same things.

Research and development for the school began in earnest and continued for more than two years. Meanwhile, the prayers continued—prayers that sustained the school's visionaries through the months of hard work, red tape, setbacks, and tedious details that come with the territory of any new venture, particularly one as ambitious as a new, innovative school.

An answer to years of prayer and hard work, New Hope Academy opened its doors in 1996, with thirty-three students in pre-kindergarten, kindergarten, and first and second grade. The school's name reflects its mission statement: "We are a community of faith. We are true believers called to shine the light of Christ into the darkest corners of despair, illuminating every heart and mind with a new vision—a new hope."

That hope continues to grow.

Today, New Hope serves more than two hundred students, in grades pre-K through sixth. The student body (representing more than 130 families) comes from a mix of Franklin's lower-, middle-, and upper-class neighborhoods. The school reserves about half of its openings for low-income students, whose full tuition is covered through donations. These students live and learn as complete equals of peers from families who can afford to pay full tuition as well as students from middle-income homes who pay partial tuition.

Almost half of New Hope's students are minorities. More than ten countries are represented. More than a quarter of the students come from single-parent homes.

New Hope operates with the belief that if both the poor and affluent remain separate we will remain impoverished and underprivileged, but together we will become empowered and enlightened, lifting one another to a Christ-centered life. Put simply, we need each other, none more important than the other.

Each school day begins with devotions and prayer, and classes are taught from a biblical worldview. With a classical approach to learning, academic excellence is required. Education is portrayed as "an atmosphere, a discipline, a life."

Perhaps just as important, these diverse students learn and grow together, across cultural, economic, and racial boundaries. Where they once saw racial or economic stereotypes, they now see friends— friends they likely would not have met if not for New Hope.

Further, kids not only learn alongside one another; they learn from one another. And as diverse students become friends, so do their parents and guardians. When needs arise, the adults who love New Hope's students jump in to meet them. Action leads to interaction. Interaction leads to friendship.

Children don't merely absorb information at New Hope; they gain the tools to free themselves from racial prejudice, economic limitations, and spiritual poverty. They graduate with the skills and the spiritual strength to be change agents in their communities and in the next phase of their educational development.

The school remains focused on the star power of each individual.

Martin Luther King Jr. once said, "I have a dream that one day . . . little black boys and black girls will be able to join hands with little white boys and white girls as sisters and brothers. . . . This is our hope. This is the faith. . . . With this faith, we will be able to work together, to pray together, to struggle together . . . knowing that we will be free one day."

Every day, New Hope is making dreams like Dr. King's come true, one child at a time, one prayer at a time.

PRAYER AND FAITH ALONE

The first and primary object of the work was, and still is, that God might be magnified by the fact that the orphans under my care are provided with all they need, only by prayer and faith, without any one being asked by me or my fellow-laborers, whereby it may be seen that God is faithful still, and hears prayer still.

—GEORGE MUELLER

AS PART OF A GRAND EXPERIMENT OF FAITH AND PRAYER, George Mueller and his associates opened an orphanage for girls seven to twelve years old on April 11, 1836, determined that they would never make any request for the needs of the orphans—except requests for prayer. An initial supply of money, furniture, beds and bedding, clothing, dishes, pots and pans, and food came in to meet the needs of the house.

Almost immediately, the needs increased. Mueller realized there were many younger girls—from age seven to infants—who needed care. And, of course, there were orphaned boys as well. Thus, Mueller opened a second home in November of 1836, then a third in September of 1837. Mueller managed these schools while also running his Scriptural Knowledge Institute and providing daily Bible instruction to local children via "day schools" he had established.

Mueller strived to run all of his efforts on faith and prayer alone. He did not want to rely on donations. But his resolve for self-sufficiency was about to face a severe test.

Lean times came to the orphanages, and Mueller and his staff spent long hours praying to God, in specific detail, about every need.

As budget shortfalls added up, Mueller strived to be a wise steward of resources. He sold anything he didn't absolutely need in order to pay rent or buy food. And his workers graciously agreed to forego their salaries for a short time.

Even these measures were not enough. At one point Mueller realized he could not pay the weekly bill for bread. So he convinced a baker to accept smaller, daily payments.

In short, Mueller and his staff did everything they could to care for the orphans. And, somehow, the children never went without food, and the orphanage never went into debt.

Income slowed to a trickle, but through the trickle, God met every need, time and again. The following story is a case in point:

One morning the plates and cups and bowls on the table were empty. There was no food in the larder, and no money to buy food.

The children were standing, waiting for their morning meal, when Mueller said, "Children, you know we must be in time for school." Lifting his hand he said, "Dear Father, we thank Thee for what Thou art going to give us to eat."

There was a knock on the door. The baker stood there and said, "Mr. Mueller, I couldn't sleep last night. Somehow I felt you didn't have bread for breakfast and the Lord wanted me to send you some. So I got up at 2 a.m. and baked some fresh bread, and have brought it."

Mueller thanked the man. No sooner had this transpired than there was a second knock at the door. It was the milkman. He announced that his milk cart had broken down right in front of the orphanage, and he would like to give the children his cans of fresh milk so he could empty his wagon and repair it.

In June of 1849, construction was completed on a building at Ashley Downs. It was able to hold three hundred children, and it quickly filled to capacity. Mueller was able to close the individual houses and bring his efforts under one roof. Eight years later, he was able to open a second large building, which housed four hundred orphans.

Five years later, 450 more orphans found a home in a third building. The year 1868 saw the opening of a fourth building, also with a capacity of 450. Home number five opened in 1870, providing care for yet another 450 children.

In 1874, Mueller wrote:

> But God, our infinite rich Treasurer, remains with us. It is this which gives me peace. Moreover if it pleases Him, with a work requiring about $264,000 a year . . . would I gladly pass through all these trials of faith with regard to means, if He only might be glorified, and His Church and the world benefited . . . I have placed myself in the position of having no means at all left; and 2,100 persons, not only daily at the table, but with everything else to be provided for, and all the funds gone; 189 missionaries to be assisted, and

nothing whatever left; about one hundred schools with 9,000 scholars in them, to be entirely supported, and no means for them in hand; about four million tracts and tens of thousands of copies of the Holy Scriptures yearly now to be sent out, and all the money expended . . . I commit the whole work to Him, and He will provide me with what I need, in future also, though I know not whence the means are to come.

Mueller was serious when he wrote of sacrificing his own means. Every year he donated almost all (85 percent) of his small salary to the cause of caring for orphans.

Over the years, Mueller saw to the housing, feeding, and raising of more than ten thousand orphans. He said in that time he had seen more than fifty thousand specific answers to prayer. He wrote:

Here is the great secret of success. Work with all your might; but trust not in the least in your work. Pray with all your might for the blessing of God; but work, at the same time, with all diligence, with all patience, with all perseverance. Pray then, and work. Work and pray. And still again pray, and then work. And so on all the days of your life. The result will surely be, abundant blessing. Whether you see much fruit or little fruit, such kind of service will be blessed.

THE ONE CONCERN OF THE DEVIL IS TO KEEP CHRISTIANS FROM PRAYING. HE FEARS NOTHING FROM PRAYERLESS STUDIES, PRAYERLESS WORK, AND PRAYERLESS RELIGION. HE LAUGHS AT OUR TOIL, MOCKS AT OUR WISDOM, BUT TREMBLES WHEN WE PRAY.
—SAMUEL CHADWICK

JEAN DRISCOLL:
THE CHAIRWOMAN
OF DEFYING THE ODDS

JEAN DRISCOLL WAS BORN WITH SPINA BIFIDA, a congenital birth defect in which the spinal column fails to close completely. Thus, doctors painted a bleak picture for Jean's parents. She would never walk. She wouldn't be able to attend traditional schools. And she would be dependent on others for the rest of her life.

Driscoll has spent her life proving those doctors wrong.

At age two, she was fitted with leg braces that allowed her to walk—although *walk* is a generous term. The young girl staggered from side to side, dragging her feet and fighting to maintain her balance. But she was moving, by her own power and determination.

As she grew older, Driscoll insisted on being included in neighborhood games, including races. She excelled at crawling through obstacle courses, and she became adept at the basketball marksmanship game of H-O-R-S-E. She developed a right-handed set shot, using her left hand to grab a fence, mailbox, or other prop for stability.

In the fourth grade, despite protests from her parents, Driscoll taught herself to ride a bike. Exhilarated by the achievement, she spent one Saturday cruising up and down a sidewalk—for eight straight hours.

Eventually, she graduated from a kid's bike with training wheels to a ten-speed. But, as a young teen, she ended up crashing that ten-speed and dislocating her left hip. She endured five operations and a year living in a body cast as she recovered. When the cast was finally removed, the hip promptly dislocated again.

Because of the accident—and her weak lower-body muscles—doctors said Driscoll would need crutches and a wheelchair to get around. And when she returned to school at age fifteen, classmates made fun of her because of the wheelchair.

Jean Driscoll was devastated. Privately, she contemplated suicide. "I couldn't make myself comfortable with the chair," she recalls, adding that even her prayers reflected her discouragement. "I would ask God, 'Why don't you pick on somebody else?' "

She tried to find herself academically, but after completing high school, she flunked out of college after three semesters.

On the social front, she didn't seek out boyfriends like her sisters did, afraid the chair would be an impossible barrier to romance and commitment. "I thought my life was over," she says flatly.

In reality, however, life was just beginning. And the hated wheelchair was the thing that got her rolling in the right direction.

At loose ends after flunking out of college, Driscoll took a job as a live-in nanny for a young family. During her year as a nanny, she met Brad Hedrick, a coach at the University of Illinois. Hedrick spoke at a wheelchair sports clinic and watched Jean and some others try their hand at a game of wheelchair soccer.

Jean Driscoll caught his eye. "I saw lots of enthusiasm and talent," he says. "Unchanneled, at the time."

Though her skill was unpolished, Hedrick took particular note of her speed. Soon, he recruited Driscoll to play wheelchair basketball at Illinois, home to the nation's top collegiate program. He didn't have to recruit very hard. His new prospect felt like she had found something that had been missing her whole life—something that came naturally to her, something she could do really well.

Driscoll went on to letter all four years for the Illini and was a three-time MVP. In her junior and senior years she led her team to the national championship. As a senior, she was named 1991's Amateur Sportswoman of the Year by the Women's Sports Foundation.

Beyond the athletic achievements, the one-time dropout graduated—with distinction—earning a bachelor's degree in speech communication. Then she went on to earn her master's in rehabilitation administration.

But even with all these accomplishments, Jean Driscoll wasn't done defying odds.

With her basketball career behind her, she turned her attention to wheelchair races, and her competitive athletic nature took over from there. She set out with a simple goal: to become the world's best wheelchair racer.

A businessman donated a racing wheelchair for her to use in her first national race, the Phoenix New Times 10K. With almost no training, she placed a respectable third. So she stepped up her training. Soon, she was winning a variety of races, nationally and internationally. At her first major international competition, in England, she won nine gold medals. Her coach, Marty Morse, encouraged her to try the marathon. She spent two years preparing to handle the longer distance, and in her first try, she finished the 1989 Chicago Marathon in under two hours (which is faster than the world record for runners).

Her Chicago performance qualified her for the prestigious Boston Marathon, where she rolled her way to a world record. And she was just getting started. The 1990 Boston debut was just the first of eight Boston Marathon victories. Her quickest Boston time, 1 hour, 34 minutes, 22 seconds, still stands as the world record.

Driscoll was relentless in her pursuit to become the world's number-one wheelchair racer. She logged as many as 130 miles every week. Her commitment to her training regimen earned her the nickname "Jean Machine" around her hometown of Champaign, Illinois. Sometimes she would invite as many as five people to latch on to her wheelchair as she powered up a steep hill.

Driscoll's early success in road races caught the attention of the U.S. Olympic team. She competed at the Olympic Games in 1992 and 1996 (where wheelchair races were exhibition events). Additionally, she made four U.S. Olympic Paralympics teams. (The Paralympics, a sister event to the traditional Olympic Games, are held in the same city as the Olympics.) Driscoll competed in a variety of distances at the 1988, 1992, 1996, and 2000 Paralympics, earning at least one gold medal each time.

In the process, she found that she was rolling right through the boundaries that once confined her. "I'm not a disabled person," she said. "I'm an elite athlete who's training for the same reasons as any other world-class athlete. I want to be the best in the world in my sport. I want to make a difference."

Driscoll retired from elite competition in 2000, after a stellar thirteen-year career. Today she speaks nationally, encouraging a variety of people to remain hopeful, even in dire circumstances. "God has given me an incredible platform," she says, "and I'm really enjoying using it. For young people and adults, the biggest limitations are the ones you place on yourself. But if you're willing to take risks, dream big, and work hard, you'll meet goals you never thought you could."

THE CIRCUMSTANCES OF OUR LIVES

HAVE AS MUCH POWER

AS WE CHOOSE TO GIVE THEM.

—DAVID MCNALLY

A WORD
OF HOPE

WHILE MEMBERS OF AN ENTEBBE, UGANDA, CHURCH PRAYED, one woman was perplexed by a strange word that had been rolling around in her head as she prayed. The word was *Kacunga*. It so impressed itself on her that she asked one of the leaders about its meaning.

The leader confessed that he wasn't familiar with *Kacunga*, but this wasn't the first time someone had asked him about that word. As the strange word found its way into the consciences of even more church members, some of them decided it was time to investigate the matter further.

They soon learned that Kacunga was an island in Lake Victoria, whose coastline runs along Entebbe's eastern edge. The group decided to send an exploratory team to the island. There, they discovered a village that had no church. So members sprung into action, forming an effort they called Victory Kings Ministries.

As Paul Masindende of Victory Kings recalls, "The island has no power, school, or hospital, and over ninety percent of the people have HIV/AIDS. But prayer is making a difference."

Indeed, fifty of the island's people quickly gave their lives to Jesus as a result of Victory Kings' efforts, and soon a church was planted.

Today, Victory Kings Ministries continues to bring transformation through God's love to Kacunga, as well as to many other of the Ssese Islands of Lake Victoria.

As Masindende notes, "Ninety-nine-point-nine percent of the Ssese Islands' people believe in witchcraft, and almost all are illiterate. So far we have reached ten islands, and we continue to pray to reach the others."

"IF I CAN DO
NOTHING ELSE,
I WILL PRAY"

LITTLE IS KNOWN OF MARIANNE ADLARD except that she was bedridden by illness and cared for by her sister. Few in her congregation knew of her except through her sister, who attended regularly. Marianne could have grown bitter at the isolation life had handed her, but instead she decided to use her hours of sitting in bed to be with God and pray instead of grousing over her condition. It was a decision that would change the lives of millions.

Sometime after Marianne had started her regular hours of prayer, Dwight L. Moody arrived in London with no more notice or fanfare than any other tourist. This was to be expected in June 1872, for no one had really heard much of D. L. Moody except as a worker in the Young Men's Christian Association (the YMCA) who had organized chaplains and evangelical outreaches to soldiers during the American Civil War. He had been to England once before to speak at a conference on Sunday schools—which at the time was a rather revolutionary outreach to the poor rather than what we know it as today.

The truth was Moody felt a bit burnt out with the ministry and was coming to England for a "spiritual sabbatical" to sit under the teaching of men like Charles Spurgeon and visit with men of faith such as George Mueller. Moody felt he needed something to re-energize his work, and so he quietly began attending meetings and taking careful notes, soaking in teaching in the churches of London simply as a listener sitting in a pew.

One night he attended a prayer meeting at the Old Bailey, a formidable building that had previously been the home of London's central criminal court but was now used as a meeting hall. When a local minister, John Lessey, who also happened to be Marianne's pastor, recognized Moody from a previous visit to England, he begged him to come to his church and speak the following Sunday. Moody told him he was there to listen, not to preach, but after much persuasion, he reluctantly agreed. He was to speak twice that day, morning and evening, and while the morning service was uneventful, the evening service was something altogether different than he had ever experienced before:

> At the next service, which was at half-past six in the evening, it seemed, while he was preaching, as if the very atmosphere was charged with the Spirit of God. There came a hush upon all the people, and a quick response to his words, though he had not been much in prayer that day, and could not understand it.
>
> When he had finished preaching he asked all who would like to become Christians to rise, that he might pray for them. People rose all over the house until it seemed as if the whole audience was getting up.

Mr. Moody said to himself. "These people don't understand me. They don't know what I mean when I ask them to rise." He had never seen such results before, and did not know what to make of it, so he put the test again.

"Now," he said, "all of you who want to become Christians just step into the inquiry-room."

They went in, and crowded the room so that they had to take in extra chairs to seat them all. The minister was surprised, and so was Mr. Moody. Neither had expected such a blessing. They had not realized that God can save by hundreds and thousands as well as by ones and twos.

After the morning service that day, Marianne's sister had gone home to tell her that Mr. Moody, from America, had preached that morning.

"I know what that means," Marianne cried. "God has heard my prayers!"

During months prior to this, as Marianne had been praying for her church, she'd come across an article about a meeting that Mr. Moody had held in the United States and cut it out. She kept the clipping under her pillow. Somehow she felt impressed that Dwight Moody was the man to bring revival to her church, so she began praying that God would send him across the ocean to preach for their congregation!

Excitedly, the healthy sister returned that night to witness the beginning of an evangelical tour that would sweep through the British Isles in the years to come.

From this start, Moody had sensed God was ready to do more in England than he had been prepared to follow through with. So after speaking at Marianne's church, he returned to Chicago to gather a small team. They returned almost a year to the day later and began a twenty-five-month tour of evangelical campaigns throughout England, Scotland, and Ireland. Moody would speak to record crowds and see tens of thousands come to Christ. In his lifetime, it is estimated that no less than one hundred million would attend a meeting to hear Dwight L. Moody preach the message of salvation.

Years later, a man by the name of G. Campbell Morgan took over the leadership of Marianne's church from Reverend Lessey, and hearing the story of her prayers, he went to meet with the bedridden sister. In his book *The Practice of Prayer*, Morgan told the following story about their encounter:

> When in 1901 I was leaving England for America I went to see her. She said to me, "I want you to reach that birthday book." I did so and turning to February 5 I saw in the handwriting I knew so well, "D. L. Moody, Psalm xci." Then Marianne Adlard said to me, "He wrote that for me when he came to see me in 1872, and I prayed for him every day until he went home." [Moody had died in December of 1899.] Continuing, she said, "Now, will you write your name on your birthday page, and let me pray for you until either you or I go home." I shall never forget writing my name in that book. To me the room was full of the Presence. I have often thought of that hour in the rush of my busy life, in the place of toil and strain, and even yet by God's good grace I know that Marianne Adlard is praying for me, and it is for this reason that to her in sincere love and admiration I have dedicated this book. There are the laborers of force in the

fields of God. It is the heroes and heroines who are out of sight, and who labor in prayer, who make it possible for those who are in sight to do their work and win. The force of it to such as are called upon to exercise the ministry can never be measured.

Seeing people come to know Jesus, it appears, is often like an iceberg. All that we see sticking above the water is the success of the minister. Yet the power that lifted them up is the 90 percent of the iceberg that is unseen beneath the water—the hours in prayer of an individual or several who stepped out of their comfort zones to believe for things others would have thought impossible.

When you pray, you must not be like the hypocrites.
For they love to stand and pray in the synagogues and
at the street corners, that they may be seen by others.
Truly, I say to you, they have received their reward.
But when you pray, go into your room and shut the door
and pray to your Father who is in secret.
And your Father who sees in secret will reward you.

—MATTHEW 6:5–6 ESV

HOPE RISES
FROM THE RUBBLE IN HAITI

COMPASSION INTERNATIONAL'S DAN WOOLLEY had just returned to his Haitian hotel after documenting the results of the ministry's Child Survival Program, which assists mothers and babies who live in severe poverty. He had learned much about survival during that day's filming and fact-finding; he was about to learn much, much more.

As he walked through the hotel lobby with a colleague, sounds like explosions erupted. The walls rippled, as if they were made of water. Desperately, he lunged for safety, losing his eyeglasses in the process.

The earthquake's damage to the Hotel Montana was devastating, as it was to much of the city of Port-au-Prince. Though severely injured, Woolley used the light on his digital camera to search for a refuge amid the ruins, wary of aftershocks and further collapsing of what remained of the hotel. He hobbled to an elevator, hoping for protection from the six layers of concrete rubble created by the quake.

In his tenuous sanctuary, Woolley, a self-described "gadget geek," used his iPhone's Pocket First Aid & CPR application to treat his injuries. He tied his shirt around the compound fracture on his leg. He secured the shirt with his belt. He stanched the blood from a severe head wound by stuffing a sock into it.

Then Woolley's attention turned to other matters. To Josh and Nate, his two young boys back home in Colorado Springs. To his wife, Christina. To God. To life and death. As hours passed, he began to realize that rescue might not be close at hand. That it might not come at all.

He did all he could to survive, including drinking his own urine to stave off dehydration. But he realized that the hours he was spending in a wrecked hotel in Haiti might be his last ones on earth. So he took out his journal and wrote messages to his family. His blood dripped on the pages as he moved his pen.

"Don't be upset at God," one message began. "He always provides for his children even in hard times. I'm still praying that God will get me out, but he may not. But even so, he will always take care of you."

When he wasn't writing messages to his family, Woolley communicated with other survivors he heard talking nearby. One of the voices he heard in the darkness was that of a Haitian bellhop. He engaged the man in conversation, eventually leading him to faith in Jesus Christ.

Meanwhile, scores of people were praying for Dan Woolley. His family. His friends. Members of his church. His colleagues at Compassion, whose sponsors and donors support more than sixty-five thousand Haitian children. And—through Compassion's international scope—people around the world prayed too, some in languages foreign to Woolley and his family.

Woolley knew, of course, that he was being supported in prayer. But he didn't know how those prayers would be answered. As Tuesday, January 12, 2010, melted into Wednesday, then Thursday, he was brought to tears by a prevailing sense that he would not survive the ordeal.

Back home, Christina was experiencing similar pain. "I knew God was holding Dan in the palm of His hand," she would tell the national media later, "but I didn't know if God was holding him in Haiti or in heaven."

On Friday morning, Christina received her answer. A search and rescue team, dispatched from Fairfax, Virginia, to Port-au-Prince, had found her husband, injured but very much alive. After sixty-five hours under the rubble, Dan Woolley was rescued. That evening he was on a plane, flying to a Miami hospital for medical treatment. When the plane touched down, his wife was waiting for him. Four days later, he was home in Colorado, hugging his sons.

"How our hearts soared," says Marti Schroeder, Dan's mother-in-law, recalling the moment the family received the good news. "We cried and laughed with joy."

While still nursing his wounds, Dan and his family patiently endured a blitz of media interest—both local and national. But whether they were talking to Meredith Vieira or a local newspaper beat writer, the family made sure that the light shined on God above anything or anyone else. "In life-and-death situations," Dan would tell anyone who would listen, "you find out what you really believe in. There were several times I was sure I was going to die. But there was never a time when I did not feel God's unmistakable presence with me."

While the Woolley family are lifetime fans of a team of life-risking rescuers from Virginia, Dan is quick to credit the ultimate Source of his rescue. "I know without a doubt," he says, his voice filling with emotion, "that I am alive today because people around the world were praying for me, by name. Not for 'the guy from Compassion,' but for Dan Woolley."

In March 2010, Dan's mother- and father-in-law sent an Easter letter to friends and family. "Our hearts cannot express . . . how grateful we are to all of you for praying for Dan," they wrote. "We do not begin to understand God's unsearchable purposes, but we are humbly grateful for His mercy in miraculously saving Dan."

The letter concludes, "As we celebrate our Lord's Passion and Resurrection, our prayer is that we would have our own hearts re-kindled with the love that Jesus has for us. And that we would re-spond to His love with a renewed devotion to love and serve Him as well as each other."

To that prayer, Dan Woolley would add his heartfelt amen.

We know that God causes everything to work together for the good of those who love God and are called according to his purpose for them.

—ROMANS 8:28 NLT

THE
ONE-MINUTE
REMIX

Followers of Jesus are not immune to times of hardship and challenges. Times when hope seems distant, out of reach. But it is really not so far away. When faced with life in a wheelchair, Jean Driscoll cried out to God in her despair. He didn't miraculously give her the ability to walk, but He gave her the strength to become a world-class athlete in that once-dreaded chair.

Jeannine Brabon's prayers—and Christlike example—helped transform a prison so notorious that it was known as the Jaws of Hell. And Dan Woolley, pulled from the earthquake rubble in Haiti after being missing for three days, will tell anyone willing to listen that he is alive today because people around the world prayed for him, by name.

Dark clouds might invade your life at times, but there is always hope in the loving God above those clouds.

A PRAYER
OF HOPE

Dear Loving God,

Help us to remember, when we begin
   to lose hope,

that all the darkness in the world

is just a speck in your light,

a light that fills the universe.

When pain and confusion invade
   our lives,

let us not rely on our own resources.

Instead, lead us to seek answers
   on our knees.

Lord, show us your way. Lord,
   lead us to your destination.

We thank you for being our beacon
   of hope,

a beacon we can always see, if we
   will only look.

Amen.

NOTES

The City of God: A City on Its Knees

"These two cities were made by two loves": Augustine of Hippo, *The City of God,* book 14, canto 28, trans. Marcus Dods (1950; repr., New York: Modern Library, 1983).

The Bittersweet Story of Alexandra

Alex's Lemonade Stand Foundation, http://www.alexslemonade.org/ (accessed June 30, 2010).

Alex's Caring Bridge Page, http://www.caringbridge.org/page/alexscott/ (accessed June 30, 2010).

Bennett, Jacqueline. "Alexandra Scott Succumbs to Cancer." *Rocky Hill Post,* August 6, 2004. http://www.zwire.com/site/index.cfm?newsid=12635694&BRD=1649&PAG=461& dept_id=11971&rfi=8 (accessed May 25, 2010).

Raich, Steve. *Girl Power.* Kansas City, MO: Hallmark Books, 2009.

"Purpose is what gives life a meaning": Charles H. Parkhurst, *The Pattern in the Mount and Other Sermons* (New York: Anson D. F. Randolph & Company, 1885), 8.

Mysterious Ways

Kuyper, Katrina and Vicki. Interview by Todd Hafer, March 2010.

One Sunday Afternoon in Birmingham, Alabama

"The result was an ugliness too well known to Americans": Martin Luther King Jr., *The Autobiography of Martin Luther King, Jr.* (New York: IPM/Warner Books, 2001), http://mlk-kpp01 .stanford.edu/kingweb/publications/autobiography/chp_19.htm (accessed May 14, 2010).

Keeping a Promise

Lakey, Jimmy. Interview by Rick Killian, March 16, 2010.

River's Promise Web site, http://www.riverspromise.com (accessed June 23, 2010).

Loose Change That Loosens Chains

Hunter, Zach. *Be the Change: Your Guide to Freeing Slaves and Changing the World.* Grand Rapids, MI: Zondervan, 2007.

"$10.5 billion lurks in American households": Coinstar Inc., coin sorting, http://www.coin .coinstar.com/coin_sorting.html (accessed May 20, 2010).

"I had all these emotions about it": ABC News, "Just 15, He Leads Fight to Abolish Slavery," *Good Morning America,* http://abcnews.go.com/GMA/story?id=2951434&page=1 (accessed May 25, 2010).

"More than twenty-seven million people worldwide": Free the Slaves, "Top Ten Facts About

Modern Slavery," http://www.freetheslaves.net/Document.Doc?id=34 (accessed May 25, 2010).

"As many as eight hundred thousand human beings": National Underground Railroad Freedom Center, "Greater Cincinnati Human Trafficking Report," http://freedomcenter.org/_media/pdf/HumanTraffickingReport.pdf (accessed May 25, 2010).

Love From the Blind Side

Amos, Joel D. "Leigh Anne Tuohy Shares Her Blind Side Story," SheKnows.com, May 30, 2010, http://www.sheknows.com/articles/812147/leigh-ann-tuohy-shares-her-blind-side-story (accessed June 10, 2010).

Lewis, Michael. *The Blind Side: Evolution of a Game.* New York: W.W. Norton, 2006.

Allyson Felix: A Runner Takes a Stand

The Official Web site of Allyson Felix, http://www.allysonfelix.com/ (accessed June 23, 2010).

Fairchild, Mary. "2008 Olympic Athlete Allyson Felix." About.com Guide. http://christianity.about.com/od/christiancelebrities/qt/allysonfelix.htm (accessed June 30, 2010).

Raich, Steve. *Girl Power.* Kansas City, MO: Hallmark Books, 2009.

Raich, Steve (founder and chairman of the board, Heart of a Champion Foundation). Interview by Todd Hafer, January and February 2009.

A Pastor Undone

iEmpathize Web site, http://www.iempathize.org (accessed June 23, 2010).

LOVE146 Web site, http://www.love146.org (accessed June 23, 2010).

Riley, Brad. Interview by Rick Killian, March 16, 2010.

"It is not more facts or statistics": Michael Hidalgo, iEmpathize *Faith and Community Promotional Brochure* (Boulder, CO: iEmpathize, 2010), 4.

The Way of the Celt

Cahill, Thomas. *How the Irish Saved Civilization: The Untold Story of Ireland's Heroic Role from the Fall of Rome to the Rise of Medieval Europe.* New York: Doubleday, 1995.

Eternal Word Television Network. "Saint Patrick Apostle of Ireland—389–461." Eternal Word Television Network. http://www.ewtn.com/library/MARY/PATRICK.HTM (accessed June 23, 2010).

"Eusebius: The Conversion of Constantine," Medieval Sourcebook, http://www.fordham.edu/halsall/source/conv-const.html (accessed June 23, 2010).

Fournier, Catherine. "Saint Patrick." Domestic-Church.com. http://www.domestic-church.com/CONTENT.DCC/19980301/SAINTS/STPAT.HTM (accessed June 23, 2010).

Hanks, Geoffrey. *70 Great Christians: The Story of the Christian Church.* Fearn, Scotland: Christian Focus Publications Ltd., 1992.

Patrick, *The Confession of Saint Patrick*, http://www.robotwisdom.com/jaj/patrick.html (accessed June 23, 2010).

Ricciotti, Giuseppe. *The Age of Martyrs: Christianity from Diocletian (284) to Constantine (337)*. Rockford, IL: Tan Books and Publishers, 1959, 1999.

Wilson, Ralph F. "Will the Real St. Patrick Please Stand Up?" Joyful Heart Renewal Ministries. http://www.joyfulheart.com/holiday/pat.htm (accessed June 23, 2010).

Becoming a Living Martyr

Grubb, Norman. *Rees Howells, Intercessor*. Fort Washington, PA: CLC Publications, 1952.

Of Poverty and Politics

Fred Outa Foundation. http://fredoutafoundation.org/ (accessed May 25, 2010).

Struck, Mark and Steward, D. Grace. "Blessed Are the Peacemakers." *Biola Magazine*. Summer 2009, 16–19.

What Love Looks Like

Perry, Michele. *Love Has a Face: Mascara, a Machete and One Woman's Miraculous Journey With Jesus in Sudan*. Grand Rapids, MI: Chosen Books, 2009.

Through New Eyes

Finney, Charles G. *The Memoirs of Reverend Charles G. Finney: Written by Himself*. New York: Fleming H. Revell Company, 1876.

"There are two kinds of means": Charles G. Finney, *Lectures on Revival of Religion*, "Prevailing Prayer," Lecture IV (New York: Leavitt, Lord & Co., 1835), 45.

"in the city of Rochester...more than one hundred thousand gave their lives to Jesus": J. Gilchrist Lawson, *Deeper Experiences of Famous Christians* (Anderson, IN: Warner Press, 1911), 243.

"On one occasion when I got to town": Paul Reno, *Daniel Nash: Prevailing Prince of Prayer* (Asheville, NC: Revival Literature, 1989), 8.

"80 percent remained strong in their faith": Lawson, *Deeper Experiences*, 243.

Chasing Little Miracles

Crowley, John. *Chasing Miracles: The Crowley Family Journey of Strength, Hope, and Joy*. New York: Newmarket Press, 2010.

Smith, Richard M. "Our Little Miracles." *Newsweek*, March 12, 2010. http://www.newsweek.com/2010/03/12/our-little-miracles.html (accessed June 30, 2010).

From Comfort to Compassion: One Teen's Story

Adapted from Walljasper, Gretchen. College application essay, Fall 2009. Used by permission.

BBC News. "Country Profile: Sierra Leone." BBC News. http://news.bbc.co.uk/2/hi/africa/country_profiles/1065898.stm (accessed July 2, 2010).

CIA World Factbook. "Sierra Leone." https://www.cia.gov/library/publications/the-world-factbook/geos/sl.html (accessed July 2, 2010).

Save the Children. "This Is Kroo Bay." SavetheChildren.org. http://www.savethechildren
.org.uk/kroobay/the_issues.php (accessed July 2, 2010).

Facing the Storms

"How is it thou hast no faith?": John Telford, *The Life of John Wesley* (London: The Epworth Press, 1924), 78.

"My brother, I must first ask you" and following dialogue: Robert Southey, *The Life of Wesley and the Rise and Progress of Methodism* (London: Frederick Warne and Company, n.d., ca. 1820), 52.

"In the evening I went very unwillingly": John Wesley, *The Journal of John Wesley*, Christian Classics Ethereal Library, http://www.ccel.org/ccel/wesley/journal.vi.ii.xvi.html (accessed May 13, 2010).

Joined by Prayer

Lukeman, Henry Augustus. "Asbury, Francis: Statue north of Meridian Hill Park in Washington, D.C." dcMemorials.com. http://dcmemorials.com/index_indiv0001822.htm (accessed May 28, 2010).

Regester, E. V., E. L. Watson, and H. K. Carroll, eds., *The Francis Asbury Monument in the National Capital*. Washington, D.C.: The Francis Asbury Memorial Association, Press of the Methodist Book Concern, 1925.

Rudolph, L. C. *Francis Asbury*. Nashville: Abingdon Press, 1966.

Salter, Darius L. *America's Bishop: The Life of Francis Asbury*. Nappanee, IN: Francis Asbury Press, 2003.

Tipple, Ezra Squier. *Francis Asbury: The Prophet of the Long Road*. New York: The Methodist Book Concern, 1916.

Searching for Nadia

CNN Wire Staff. "God 'Led Me Directly' to Girl Lost in Swamp, Florida Rescuer Says." CNN.com. http://www.cnn.com/2010/US/04/14/florida.girl.rescued/index.html?iref=allsearch (accessed May 25, 2010).

WESH News, "Church Member Finds Nadia Bloom in Dense Woods," WESH.com. http://www.wesh.com/video/23139564/index.html (accessed May 25, 2010).

Awakening

"Morality and religion in Britain have collapsed": George Berkeley, *Discourse to Magistrates and Men in Authority* (Dublin: George Faulkner, 1738).

"broke out with one voice": John Wesley, *The Journal of John Wesley*, vol. 2, ed. Nehemiah Curnock (London: Epworth Publishing, 1938), 122–125, quoted in Eddie L. Hyatt, *2000 Years of Charismatic Christianity: A 20th Century Look at Church History from a Pentecostal/Charismatic Perspective* (Chicota, TX: Hyatt International Ministries, Inc., 1996), 106.

"I would give a hundred guineas": Harry S. Stout, "Heavenly Comet," *Christian History* 12, no. 2 [Issue 38] (1993): 10.

"Give Me Souls, O God, or I Die!"

"Are you praying for quickening in your own life" and following questions: E. G. Carre (ed.), *Praying Hyde: The Life Story of John Hyde* (Orlando: Bridge Logos, 1982), 9–10.

"He would engage a man in a talk about his salvation": Ibid., 27.

The Disarming Power of Peace

Story adapted from Goleman, Daniel. *Emotional Intelligence: Why It Can Matter More Than IQ.* New York: Bantam Books, 1995.

Charles Spurgeon's Five Hundred Children

Fullerton, W. Y. "Charles Haddon Spurgeon: A Biography." The Spurgeon Archive. http://spurgeon.org/misc/biopref.htm (and subsequent links) (accessed July 1, 2010).

"it would take four souls the size of yours" story: James William Cox, ed., *The Ministers Manual* 1995 ed. (San Francisco: HarperSanFrancisco, 1994), 346.

Prayer and Lightning

Cogswell, William. *Letters to Young Men Preparing for the Christian Ministry.* Boston: Perkins & Marvin, 1837.

Harman, Mac. "The Haystack Prayer Meeting," Williams College. http://wso.williams.edu/~dchu/MissionPark/meeting.html (and subsequent links) (accessed May 25, 2010).

Collegiate Day of Prayer, "History of Collegiate Prayer," Collegiate Day of Prayer, http://www.collegiatedayofprayer.org/history.html (and subsequent links) (accessed May 25, 2010).

"In the year 1823": Henry C. Fish, *Handbook of Revivals* (Boston: J. H. Earle, 1874), 297.

Prayers That Changed the Fate of Nations

"A man ought to look": August Gottlieb Spangenberg, *The Life of Nicholas Lewis Count Zinzendorf* (London: Samuel Holdsworth, 1838), 43.

"a day of the outpourings": Dr. A. K. Curtis, "A Golden Summer," Zinzendorf Jubilee, Comenius Foundation, http://www.zinzendorf.com/agolden.htm (accessed May 13, 2010). This article first appeared in *Glimpses of Christian History*, "Glimpses 37: Zinzendorf," from the Christian History Institute.

"Prayer itself is an art": Charles Spurgeon, "Order and Argument in Prayer" (sermon, Metropolitan Tabernacle, Newington, London, July 15, 1866), *Metropolitan Tabernacle Pulpit*, vol. 12, no. 700, http://www.spurgeon.org/sermons/0700.htm (accessed May 24, 2010).

A One-Way Ticket

Bombay Teen Challenge. http://bombayteenchallenge.org/ (accessed July 2, 2010).

Devaraj, K. K. Interview by Rick Killian, June 18, 2010.

From Small Beginnings

"There is no party spirit": Keith Malcomson, "The 1859 Ulster Revival," *Heaven Sent Revival*

Publications, http://www.pentecostalpioneers.org/UlsterRevival1859.html (accessed May 18, 2010).

"the positive contribution made": UK Citizens Online Democracy, "1859 Revival Anniversary Debate," Northern Ireland Assembly, November 4, 2008, http://www.theyworkforyou.com/ni/?id=2008-11-04.4.1 (accessed May 13, 2010).

"By the end of 1860": Ibid.

The Clapham Conspiracy

Colson, Charles. *Kingdoms in Conflict: An Insider's Challenging View of Politics, Power, and the Pulpit.* Grand Rapids, MI: Zondervan, 1987.

Hill, Clifford. *The Wilberforce Connection.* London: Monarch Books, 2004.

"God Almighty has set before me two great objects": Robert Isaac and Samuel Wilberforce, eds, *The Correspondence of William Wilberforce,* vol. 1 (London: John Murray, 1838), 149, quoted in Hill, *The Wilberforce Connection,* 49.

"I saw what seemed a mere shrimp": "Sickly shrimp of a man who sank the slave ships" *Sunday Times Online* (March 25, 2007), http://www.timesonline.co.uk/tol/life_and_style/men/article1563804.ece (accessed June 30, 2010).

"I am certain I risk nothing": Hennell, Michael, *John Venn and the Clapham Sect* (London: Lutterworth Press, 1958), 203.

"An Appointment With God"

Story adapted from "Transformation, Obedience and Prayer: A Moving True Story." 24-7 Prayer. http://www.24-7prayer.com/features/753 (accessed June 23, 2010). Used by permission.

A Miracle on Fulton Street

America's Great Revivals: The Story of Spiritual Revival in the United States, 1734–1899. Minneapolis: Bethany House, 2004.

"This winter of 1857–58 will be remembered": Charles Finney, *The Memoirs of Reverend Charles G. Finney: Written by Himself* (New York: Fleming H. Revell Company, 1876), 442.

The White Rose

Junge, Traudl. *Blind Spot: Hitler's Secretary,* DVD. Directed by André Heller and Othmar Schmiderer. Culver City, CA: Sony Pictures, 2002.

"was against God's commandments": Annette E. Dumbach and Jud Newborn, *Shattering the German Night: The Story of the White Rose* (New York: Little, Brown, and Company, 1986), quoted in Vicky Knickerbocker, *Study Guide for Sophie Scholl: The Final Days* (Minneapolis: Outreach Coordinator at the Center for Holocaust and Genocide Studies, University of Minnesota, 2006), 4.

"Shaken and broken": Society of the White Rose, *Fellow Fighters in the Resistance!,* http://www.katjasdacha.com/whiterose/leaflets/E6.html (accessed May 13, 2010).

"Then a woman prison guard brought in Sophie": Richard Hanser, *A Noble Treason* (New York: G.P. Putnam's Sons, 1979), 279–280.

"Now, my death will be easy and joyful": Jacob G. Hornberger, "The White Rose: A Lesson in Dissent," Jewish Virtual Library, http://www.jewishvirtuallibrary.org/jsource/Holocaust/rose.html (accessed May 13, 2010).

Into the Jaws of Hell

Alford, Deann. "New Life in a Culture of Death." *Christianity Today*, February 1, 2004. http://www.christianitytoday.com/ct/2004/february/5.48.html (accessed June 30, 2010).

Crouse, Janice Shaw. "Jeannine Brabon's Ministry in Colombia's Jaws of Hell," *Great Cloud of Witnesses*. Ed. Jack Voelkel. Urbana Ministries. http://www.urbana.org/great-cloud-of-witnesses/jeannine-brabons-ministry-in-colombias-jaws-of-hell (accessed May 24, 2010).

Pitts, Dan. Interview by Todd Hafer, February 3, 2010, and March 16, 2010.

When the End Is the Beginning

Athletes for Hope. "Andrea Jaeger." http://www.athletesforhope.org/andreajaeger.html (accessed June 30, 2010).

Raich, Steve (founder and chairman of the board, Heart of a Champion Foundation). Interview by Todd Hafer, January and February 2009.

New Hope Academy: A "City on Our Knees" Goes to School

Education.com. Tennessee Schools. http://www.education.com/schoolfinder/us/tennessee/ (accessed May 25, 2010).

McKeehan, Toby. Interview by Todd Hafer, February 3, 2010, and March 16, 2010.

New Hope Academy Web site, http://www.nhafranklin.org/ (accessed June 30, 2010).

Pitts, Dan. Interview by Todd Hafer, February 3, 2010, and March 16, 2010.

Private School Review, New Hope Academy page, http://www.privateschoolreview.com/school_ov/school_id/26217 (accessed May 25, 2010).

"I have a dream": Martin Luther King Jr., "I Have a Dream," address at March on Washington, August 28, 1963, Washington, D.C., http://www.mlkonline.net/dream.html (accessed May 25, 2010).

Prayer and Faith Alone

Mueller, George. *The Life of Trust: Being a Narrative of the Lord's Dealings with George Mueller, Written by Himself*. Boston: Gould and Lincoln, 1868.

Story of God's provision of bread and milk for breakfast: Ed Reese, *The Life and Ministry of George Mueller* (Lansing, IL: Reese Publications, n.d.), http://www.uvm.edu/~sbross/biography/muller.txt (accessed March 11, 2010).

"But God, our infinite rich Treasurer": Ibid.

"Here is the great secret of success": Arthur T. Pierson, *George Mueller of Bristol* (Old Tappan, NJ: Fleming H. Revell Company, 1899), http://www.fbinstitute.com/Mueller/George_Mueller_Bristol_Tex.html (accessed May 18, 2010).

Jean Driscoll: The Chairwoman of Defying the Odds

Jean Driscoll Web site, http://www.jeandriscoll.com/ (accessed June 30, 2010).

Raich, Steve (founder and chairman of the board, Heart of a Champion Foundation). Interview by Todd Hafer, January and February 2009.

"The circumstances of our lives": David McNally, *The Eagle's Secret: Success Strategies for Thriving at Work & in Life* (New York: Delacorte Press, 1998), 3.

A Word of Hope

Hardy, Carla. "Intercessors Called to Un-churched Ugandan Island," 24-7 Prayer. http://www.24-7prayer.com/content/834 (accessed May 14, 2010). Used by permission.

"If I Can Do Nothing Else, I Will Pray"

"At the next service, which was half-past six in the evening": William R. Moody, *The Life of Dwight L. Moody* (New York: Fleming H. Revell Company, 1900), 152–153.

"God has heard my prayers!": Ibid., 153–154.

"When in 1901 I was leaving England for America": G. Campbell Morgan, *The Practice of Prayer* (London: Hodder and Stoughton, 1906), 124–127.

Hope Rises From the Rubble in Haiti

Jones, Leura. "Haiti After the Earthquake." Compassion.com. http://www.compassion.com/sponsordonor/countrynews/ha/Stories/haiti-after-the-earthquake.htm (accessed June 30, 2010).

Woolley, Dan. Interview by Todd Hafer, April 2010.

Schroeder, Marti. Easter letter to family and friends, April 2010.

Schroeder, Marti. Interview by Todd Hafer, April and May 2010.

ABOUT THE ARTIST

TobyMac is a Grammy Award–winning artist, producer, and songwriter. First known as part of the popular group dc Talk throughout the 1990s, he launched a solo career in 2001 and has since won numerous awards, earned three certified gold albums, and had six No. 1 CHR singles. "City on Our Knees," the inspiration for this book, spent thirteen weeks as Billboard's No. 1 Christian song. TobyMac's previous books include *Jesus Freaks* (with dc Talk) and *Under God* (with Michael Tait and WallBuilders). TobyMac is married, with five children, and makes his home near Nashville, Tennessee.